RSL 11+ M

This book contains **six papers of increasing difficulty**, ranging from ISEB (Independent Schools Examination Board) standard to the level of the most competitive schools. The tests are accompanied by detailed, *teaching* mark schemes, designed to communicate the most important exam skills to students of all abilities.

The solution pages aim to clearly demonstrate the skills needed for each question, very much as I explain them to my own pupils. Some students will be able to follow the solutions independently, but they have been created with a supportive adult in mind.

Please bear in mind that the example solutions are *no more than suggestions*. Very few of them claim to be the only possible approach. For reasons of space, some possible methods have inevitably not been included here.

As the book goes on, the solutions return less frequently to basic methods, in order to avoid duplication. However, frequent cross-references will direct you to places earlier in the book where methods are explained more fully.

Although these papers have been designed carefully in response to the exams set by many schools in recent years, they cannot attempt to imitate every design of test, and they are not predictive. Sometimes a school sets another sort of exam: for example, a multiple-choice test. However, the essential skills of analysing a question and providing clear working, demonstrated throughout these papers, will be useful preparation for any maths exam based on the Key Stage 2 syllabus.

If you find these materials useful, you might be interested in reading about my *11 Plus Lifeline* service at **www.11pluslifeline.com**, which offers printable resources for all 11+ subjects.

How To Use This Book: Advice For Students

These materials can be used in different ways. For example, you may wish to answer some papers while reading the solutions, in order to understand how an exam works. However, most people will choose to write their answers then refer to the marking sheet.

When you are correcting your work, it is a good idea to take notes of any important points: this will help you to remember them. If your answer could be improved, it is often worth repeating it with reference to the mark scheme.

These papers will be most useful if you complete them in order. Although each test and mark sheet can stand alone, used in sequence they will build up your skills steadily.

The papers in this book have been designed for use without time limits, because they are focused on teaching each student to produce skilful, carefully reasoned answers. When these skills have been acquired, it is usually a fairly simple matter to speed them up with the practice papers available from many schools or through 11 Plus Lifeline. Timing problems are almost always caused by a lack of confidence with core techniques.

A Guide To Marking

- ✓ A correct answer with correct units (£, kg, etc.) will get full marks irrespective of the student's working out (or lack of it), unless the question directly asks for working to be provided.

- ✓ A mark should be deducted for missing units (half a mark if it is a one-mark question).

- ✓ If the answer is slightly wrong but the working is almost completely correct, deduct only one mark. (Bear in mind that your working might be different from my suggested method in the answer pages, but still be valid.)

- ✓ If the answer is wrong and the working is substantially wrong, look for correct moments in the working: for example, the first stage of the method is right, after which it veers off course. Correct moments in a substantially wrong answer might together be worth up to half a mark in a two-mark question, one mark in a three-mark question, two marks in a four-mark question, and so on.

- ✓ If an answer involves drawing, deduct marks when the drawing is so messy or inaccurate that the answer can no longer reasonably be called correct – for example, if a line does not pass through a specified coordinate, or if it is supposed to be straight but bends noticeably.

Follow-through marking: If the answer to part (b) of a question (for example) depends on an incorrect answer from part (a), but is otherwise correct, award (b) full marks.

Also Available

11 Plus Lifeline (printable resources for all 11+ subjects): **www.11pluslifeline.com**

RSL Creative Writing (several volumes)

RSL 11+ Comprehension: Volumes 1 & 2
RSL 8+ to 10+ Comprehension
RSL 13+ Comprehension

GCSE Maths by RSL, Higher Level (9-1), Non-Calculator
GCSE Spanish by RSL
GCSE French by RSL
GCSE German by RSL

Contents

1. *Balloon Over Peril Island*   standard level   5

       Guidance and solutions   18

2. *Wei Wei's Pies*   standard level   42

       Guidance and solutions   54

3. *Wazzoo!*   challenging level   70

       Guidance and solutions   82

4. *Roderick the Cart Horse*   challenging level   98

       Guidance and solutions   110

5. *Mr Biggles*   advanced level   126

       Guidance and solutions   138

6. *Goblins in the Casino Royale*   advanced level   158

       Guidance and solutions   172

We are a family business in a competitive marketplace. We want to improve and expand our range, providing even better products for our customers, including families who may not wish to purchase long courses of private tuition. If you have any feedback, please let me know! My email address is **robert@rsleducational.co.uk**.

If you like this book, please tell your friends and write a review on Amazon!

RSL 11+ Maths (3rd edition)

by Robert Lomax

Published by RSL Educational Ltd

Copyright © RSL Educational Ltd 2021

Company 10793232

VAT 252515326

Registered in England & Wales

Cover design by Heather Macpherson at Raspberry Creative Type

Image on 11 Plus Lifeline information page © iStockPhoto.com.

Cover images & graphics © Shutterstock.com.

www.rsleducational.co.uk

Photocopying more than four pages of this book is not permitted, even if you have a CLA licence. Extra copies are available from www.rsleducational.co.uk and from Amazon.

Paper 1: *Balloon Over Peril Island*

Standard Level

Papers 1 and 2 are similar to the exams set by the Independent Schools Examination Board (ISEB), and at a comparable level to many grammar school 11+ papers. They require students to demonstrate core skills from across the Key Stage 2 syllabus. There is less emphasis on lateral thinking than in the more demanding papers later in this pack.

---

1. **(a)** Write down the product of 6 and 7.

Answer: .... **(1)**

(b) What is the remainder when 728 is divided by 9?

Answer: .... **(2)**

(c) Subtract –11 from –9.

Answer: .... **(2)**

(d) Write down a factor of 14.

Answer: .... **(1)**

---

2. There are 2459 jellybeans in my rucksack.

(a) **(i)** How many jellybeans do I have, correct to the nearest 100?

Answer: .... **(1)**

(ii) What is the value of the 5 in 2459?

Answer: .... **(1)**

Oscar eats so many jellybeans that he feels ill. Gretel eats 46 jellybeans. There are 1912 jellybeans left.

(b) How many jellybeans does Oscar eat?

Answer: .... **(2)**

3.   Here is a number pattern, with two numbers missing:

   6   13   __   27   34   __

   (a) From the four numbers given above, write down:

   (i) a prime number   Answer: ………………   **(1)**

   (ii) a multiple of 9   Answer: ………………   **(1)**

   (iii) two numbers with a difference of 28

                                    Answer: ………………   **(1)**

   (iv) two numbers whose product is 78

                                    Answer: ………………   **(1)**

   (b) Write down the two missing numbers.   Answer: ……..   ……..   **(2)**

   (c) Find the mean of all six numbers in the pattern.

                                    Answer: ………………   **(2)**

4.

PEANUTS FOR SALE!
£1.80 for 100g
£10 for 1kg

   (a) Rahim sees this sign and decides to buy a 100g bag for each of his 3 children.

   (i) How much does he spend?

                                    Answer: ………………   **(2)**

   (ii) He pays with a £20 note. How much change does he get back?

                                    Answer: ………………   **(2)**

(b) Agatha wants to buy 1200g of peanuts for as little money as possible. How much does she spend?

Answer: ……………… **(3)**

5. Ulrika Megablag, an estate agent, is carrying out a survey to discover whether people without gardens are interested in moving house. She asks 100 people whether they have a garden, and whether they are interested in moving house.

Here are her results as a Venn diagram. One number ('?') is missing:

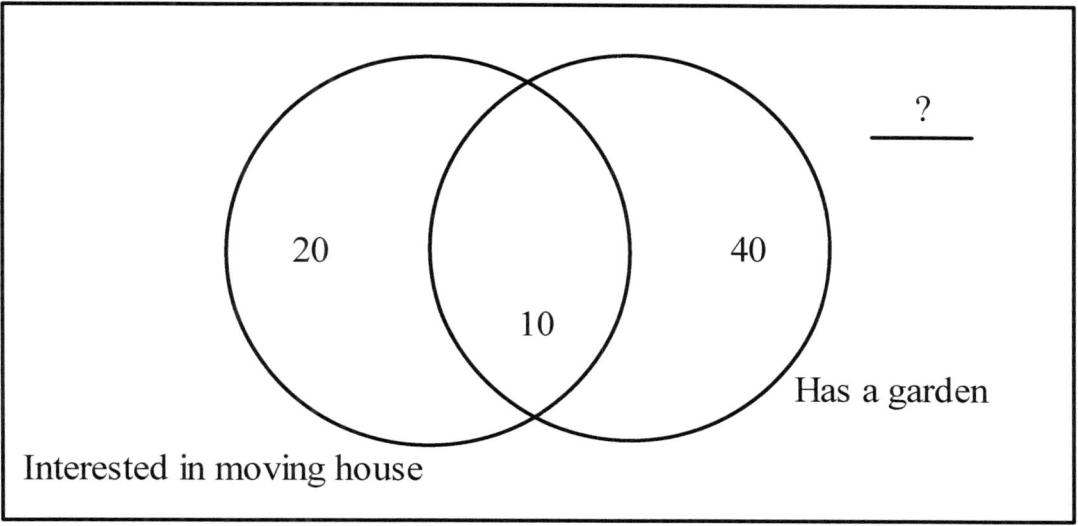

(a) Based on the Venn diagram above, complete the following table by writing the correct number in each box: **(4)**

	Has a Garden	Does Not Have a Garden
Interested in Moving House		
Not Interested in Moving House		

(b) Ulrika wanted to find out whether people without a garden are interested in moving house. What answer do her survey results suggest?

Answer: ....

....

....

.... **(2)**

---

6. **(a)** Plot the following three points on the centimetre grid below:

    (1, 7)   (6, 2)   (1, 5) **(2)**

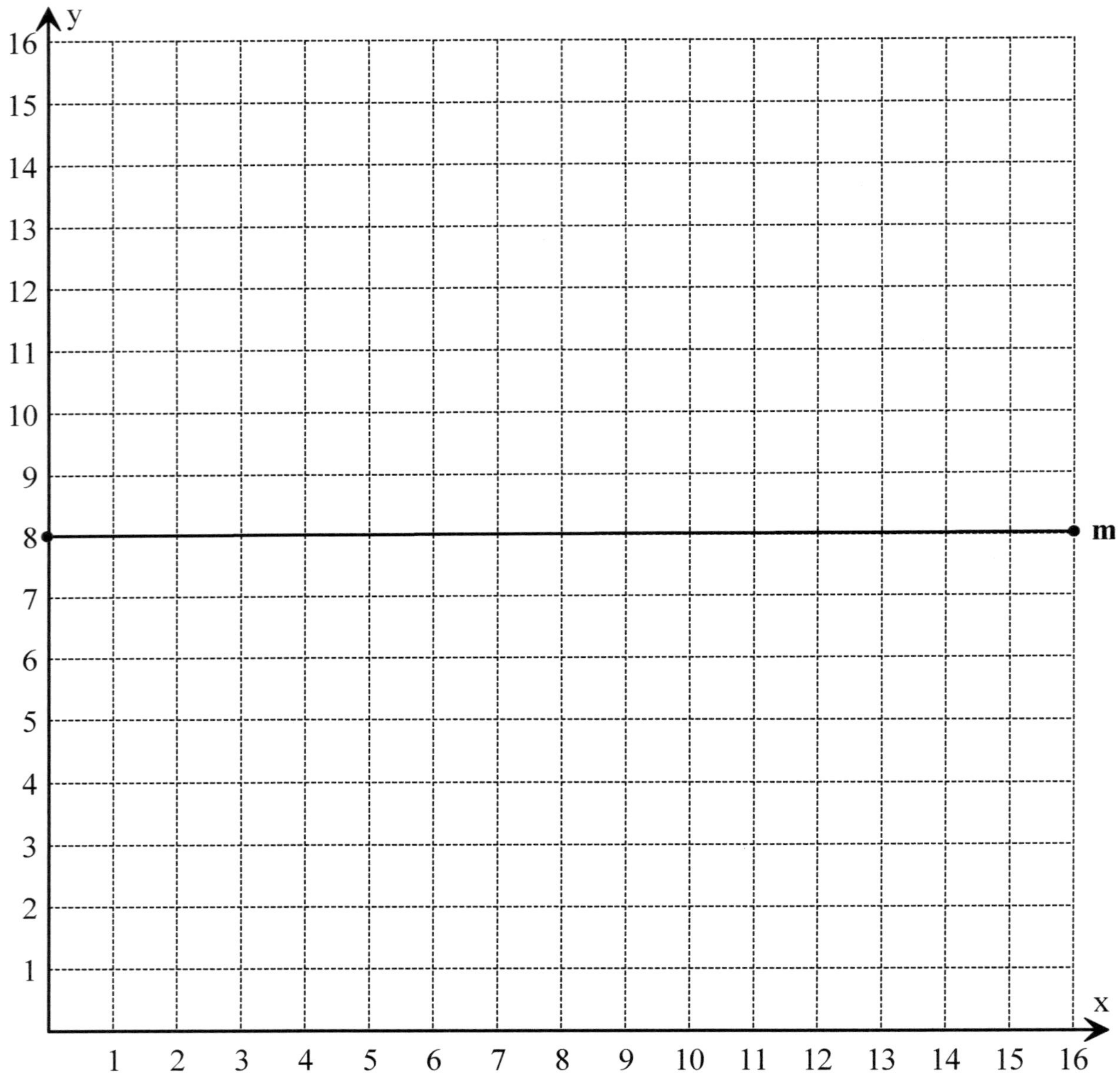

(b) **(i)** Add another point so that the four points together form a **parallelogram**. Label the shape **P**. **(1)**

(ii) Write down the coordinates of your new point.

Answer: (…….. , ……) **(2)**

(iii) What is the order of rotational symmetry of shape **P**?

Answer: ……………… **(1)**

(c) Reflect shape **P** in the mirror line, **m**. Label your new shape **N**. **(2)**

(d) Translate shape **P** 8 cm to the right and 3 cm up. Label your new shape **S**. **(2)**

(e) What is the area of shape **S**?

Answer: ………… cm² **(2)**

---

7. Claire and Darren interviewed 48 football supporters from their school, in order to find out what the most popular Premiership football teams were.

The following frequency table shows their results:

Team	Frequency
Manchester United	9
Liverpool	5
Everton	4
Leicester City	17
Manchester City	12
Newcastle	1

(a) Complete the bar graph below, using the information from the frequency table. One bar has been done for you. **(4)**

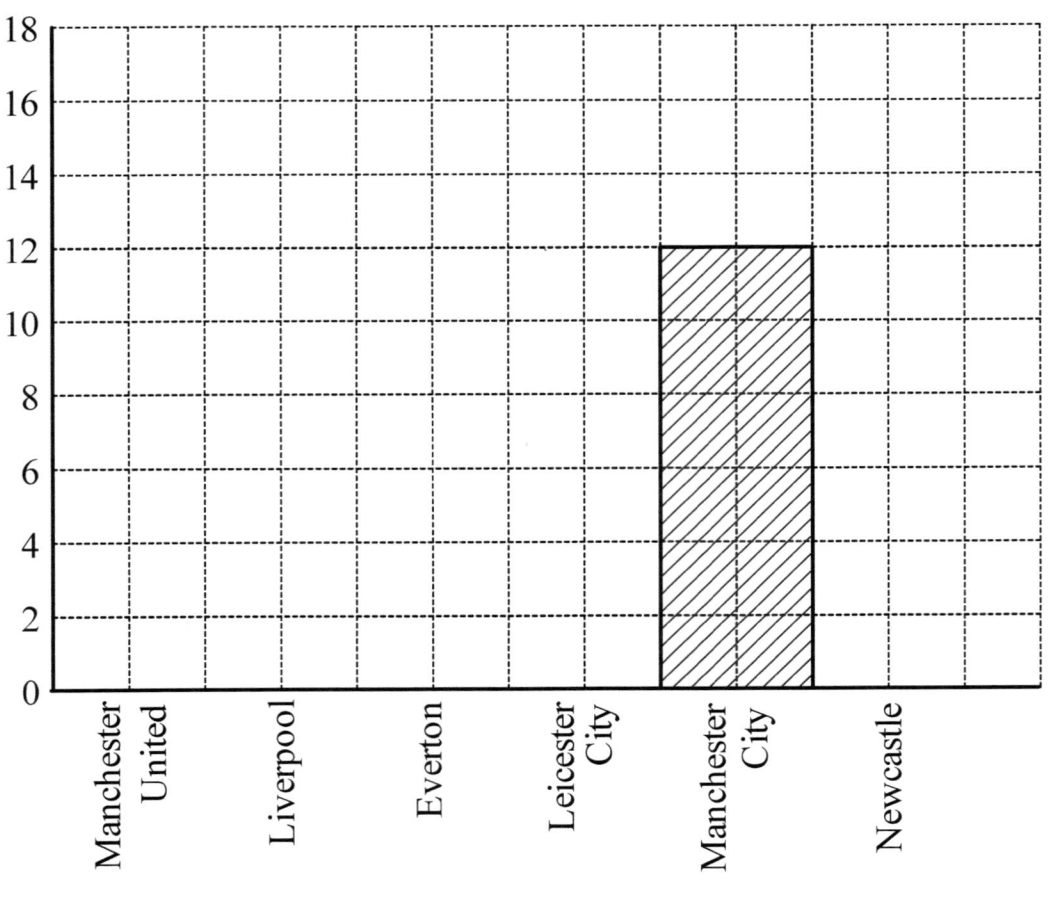

(b) **(i)** What is the range of the frequencies?

Answer: ……………. **(1)**

(ii) What is the mean number of supporters per team?

Answer: ……………. **(2)**

(iii) What is the median number of supporters?

Answer: ……………. **(2)**

(c) After Darren and Claire have completed their graph, some more students approach them, saying that they all support Arsenal. Claire realises that if they add this data to their graph, the mean will not change.

How many people support Arsenal?

Answer: ……………. **(2)**

8.   Alex lives 900 metres from his school.

   (a) One day he is late, so he runs the first $\frac{2}{5}$ of his journey.

   (i) How far does he run?

                                                          Answer: ……………   **(2)**

   (ii) What percentage of the journey does he have left?

                                                          Answer: ……………   **(1)**

   (b) Another day he runs 15% of the journey. How far does he run in metres?

                                                          Answer: ……………   **(2)**

---

9.   Write these fractions in order, starting with the smallest:

   $$\frac{1}{3} \quad \frac{2}{5} \quad \frac{3}{10} \quad \frac{3}{8} \quad \frac{1}{2}$$

         Answer: …….. …….. …….. …….. ……..   **(3)**

10. Victor is going to ask me some questions. If I get the answer wrong, he will win some of my jellybeans. I do not want to give away my jellybeans. What answer should I give to each question?

(a) I take a number, multiply it by 7 and subtract 11. My answer is 73. What number did I start with?

Answer: …………….. **(2)**

(b) I divide a number by 5 then square the result, and my answer is 64. What number did I start with?

Answer: …………….. **(2)**

(c) Based on the following facts, what is my number?

- It is a prime number.
- It is over 18.
- It is a factor of 69.

Answer: …………….. **(2)**

(d) I multiply a number by 6, subtract 12, then divide by 2. I end up with twice my original number. What number did I start with?

Answer: …………….. **(3)**

---

11. Reflect each of these three shapes in its mirror line:

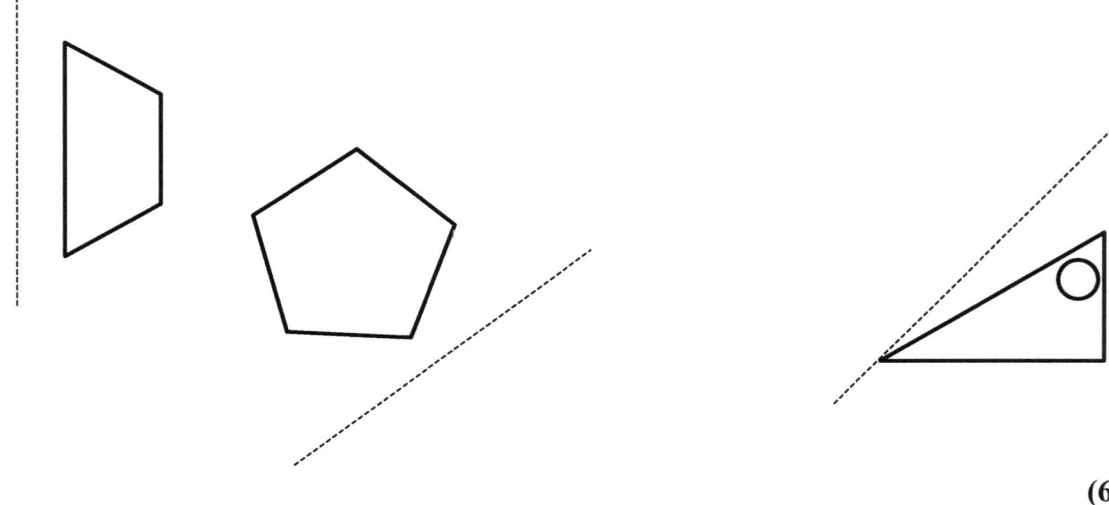

(6)

12. The line graph below gives the cost of taking a hot air balloon ride with Neardeath Experiences:

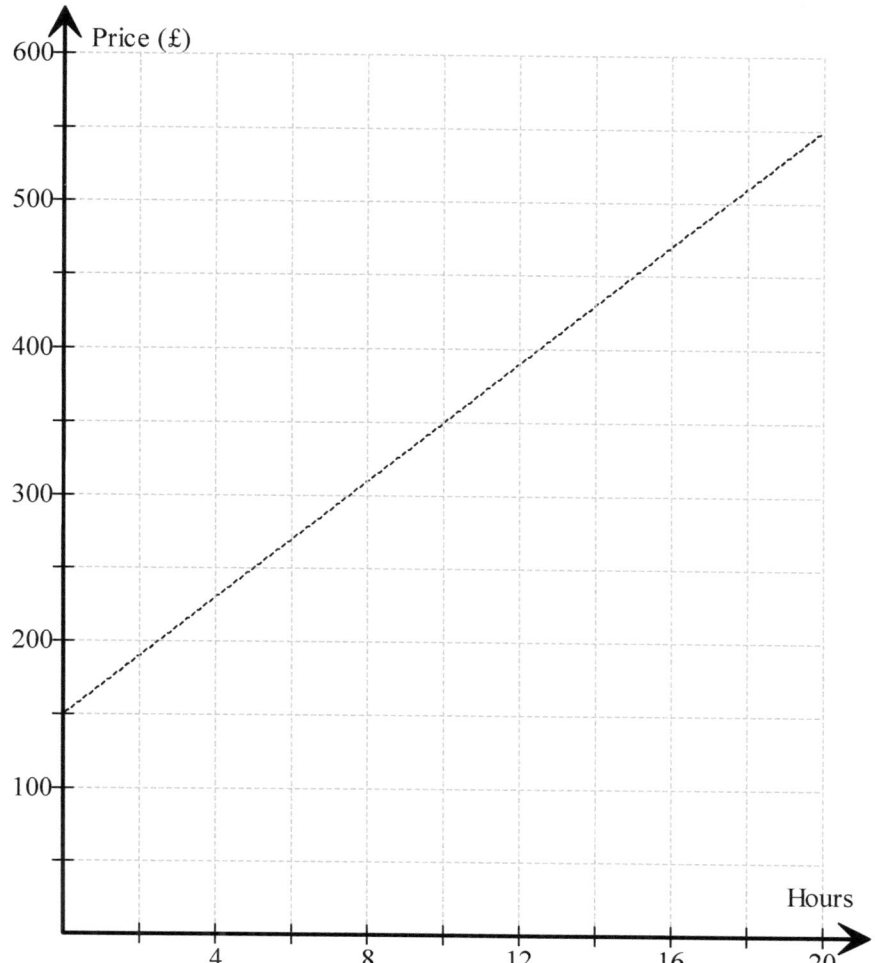

(a) (i) A balloon trip cost me £500. How long did it last?

Answer: .... (2)

(ii) How much would it cost to travel in the balloon for 12 hours?

Answer: .... (2)

(b) Sandra and Elaine pay £100 for 2 hours in a balloon. Did they travel with Neardeath Experiences? Explain your answer.

Answer: ....

....

....

.... (2)

13. Captain Mizzenmast, the ruthless pirate, is hunting for the buried treasure of Peril Island. In his pocket he has some secret instructions:

Secret Instructions

From Skullmaggot Cove send your sea-legs 2 km west, then 1 km north, then 500 metres south-east.

There lie riches beyond the dreams of man …

… and this map of Peril Island, which does not show the treasure:

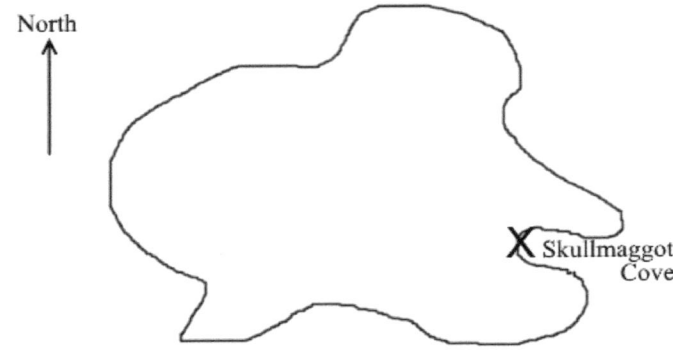

(a) Following the Secret Instructions above and using a scale of 2 cm to represent 1 km, accurately locate the treasure on the map. (3)

(b) Captain Mizzenmast decides to walk directly to the treasure from Skullmaggot Cove.

    (i) Draw this route on the map. (1)

    (ii) How far is this direct journey, to the nearest 0.5 km?

Answer: ……………. (2)

(iii) Cutting their way straight through the jungle, the Captain and his crew travel at 1.5 km per hour.

Using your answer to **(ii)**, calculate how long this journey will take.

Answer: …… hrs …… mins   **(3)**

---

14. The following sheet of newspaper is used to wrap my fish and chips. How many pages were there in the complete paper?

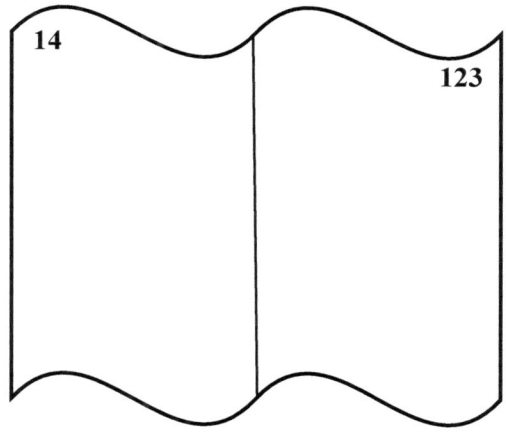

Answer: ……………   **(3)**

15. In a magic square, each row, column and diagonal has the same total.

   Complete the following magic square, using every number from 3 to 11:

4	11	
	3	10

   (5)

TOTAL MARKS: 100

youtube.com/c/Easy11Plus

Paper 1: Balloon Over Peril Island

Solutions

1. (a) The **product** is what you get when you **multiply** numbers together – like what you 'produce' when you mix ingredients.

$$6 \times 7 = \underline{\underline{42}}$$

(b)

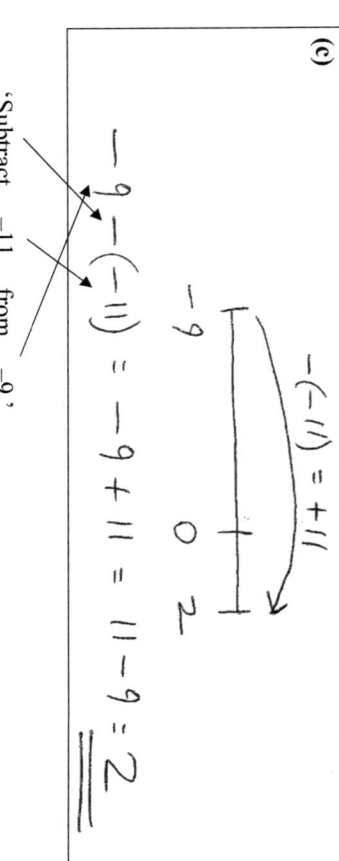

In other words, how much is left 'spare' when you have squeezed the greatest possible number of 9s into 728?

(c) 'Subtract −11 from −9.'

'From' in effect swaps the order of the two numbers.

The crucial thing to remember here is that '**minus minus = plus**': in this case, **minus minus 11 = plus 11**, or −(−11) = +11.

$$-9 - (-11) = -9 + 11 = 11 - 9 = \underline{\underline{2}}$$

Number lines are a wonderful way of making negative numbers clear, if you stick to the basic principle that **minus moves left and plus moves right**. Look at the example above:

- Start at −9.
- −(−11) means +11, so move **right** 11 places …
- … and land on 2, which is the answer.

Notice that −9 + 11 is the same as 11 − 9, which might make life easier!

(d) A **factor** is any (whole) number which, **when multiplied by another** (whole) number, gives the number you are looking for.

- 1 and 14 are factors of 14 because 1 × 14 = 14
- 2 and 7 are factors of 14 because 2 × 7 = 14

$$\underline{\underline{1 \text{ or } 2 \text{ or } 7 \text{ or } 14}}$$

2. (a) (i)

24(5)9 therefore 2500

The upwards arrow is showing that **50 or above rounds up** to the next hundred.

(ii)

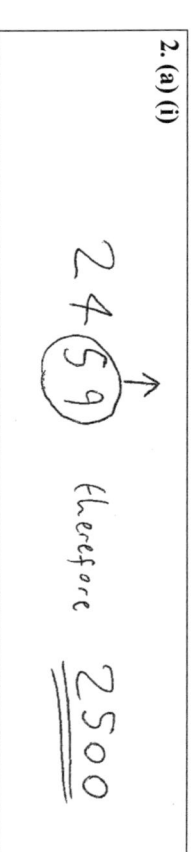

(b)

$$\begin{array}{r}\cancel{5}\cancel{4}\cancel{5}9 \text{ (original number)} \\ -1912 \text{ (leftovers)} \\ \hline 547 \text{ (number eaten)}\end{array}$$

$$\begin{array}{r}547 \text{ (total eaten)} \\ -46 \text{ (Gretel's share)} \\ \hline 501 \text{ Oscar's share}\end{array}$$

501

RSL Educational does not endorse the eating of 501 jellybeans. I prefer not to disclose whether this is question is based on personal experience.

---

3. (a) (i)   **13**

A **prime number** has **no factors** (see **Q1(c)** above) **except for itself and 1**.

For example:
- 1 and 18 are factors of 18, but so are 2 and 9 (2 × 9 = 18), so 18 is **not** prime.
- 1 and 17 are factors of 17, and it has no other factors, so 17 **is** prime.
-

(ii) $3 \times 9 = 27$

A **multiple** of a number is produced when you **multiply** that number by another whole number (the words 'multiple' and 'multiply' are very similar).

Do not confuse **multiples** and **factors**!

(iii)

$$34 - 6 = 28$$

34 and 6

Difference means **how far apart** two numbers are. You find this by **subtracting** the smaller number from the larger.

(iv)   **6 and 13**

See **Q1(a)** above.

(b)

6   13   20   27   34   41
 ↑7↓   20 and 41

- **Count the gaps** between the pairs of numbers given in the question.
- Because the two differences are the same, it is likely that the difference of 7 continues all the way through the sequence.
- Try following this rule, and then check that your numbers do indeed fit.

(c)

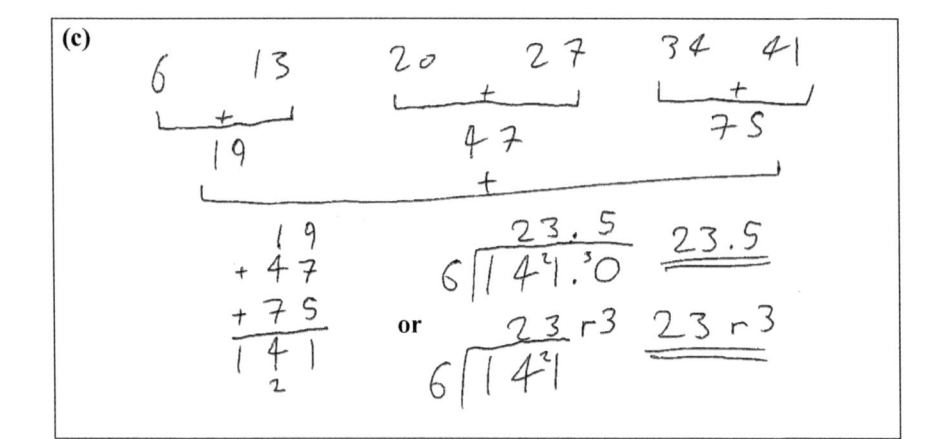

```
   6   13    20   27   34   41
    \_/  \_/  \_/  \_/  \_/
    19    47    75
```

```
    19
  + 47
  + 75
  ---
   141
```

The **mean** is often referred to as the 'average' (but be careful: a **median** is also a form of average).

You find the mean by

- **finding the total** of the numbers (141);
- **dividing** this by the **number of numbers** you originally had (6).

```
      23.5              23 r3
    _____           _____
  6|141.30    or    6|141
                         
                      23 r3
                     _____
                    6|141
```

Because the answer (23.5) lies between 20 and 27, the middle numbers in the sequence, common sense says that it is likely to be correct.

Notice how the example adds the numbers in pairs before combining the results – a useful way to avoid adding six numbers at once.

- This is an example of a question which should be marked using the 'follow-through' method: if your answer to **(b)** was wrong, **(c)** should be marked based on the answer you gave. A correctly calculated mean, even if based on the wrong numbers, still gets the marks.

---

4. (a) (i)

```
    1.80
  ×    3
  -----
    5.40
      2
```

£5.40

- Count the digits to the right of all decimal points above the line:

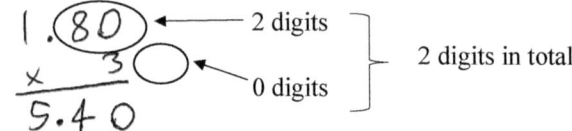

  1.80 ← 2 digits
  × 3 ← 0 digits
  -----
         2 digits in total

- Below the line, count back the same number of places from the right hand end, and write the decimal point:

  1.80
  × 3

  5.4̄0
     2 1

(ii)

```
    1.80
  ×    3
  -----
    5.40
      2
```

```
     9
   2̶0̶.¹0 0
  -  5. 4 0
  ---------
    1 4. 6 0
```

£14.60

When you **subtract**, you must **line up the decimal** points (unlike when you multiply), adding zeros afterwards if necessary. Using pounds and pence helps, as above.

(b)

```
  1200g = 1kg + 100g + 100g
         £10 + £1.80 + £1.80
       = £10 + £3.60 = £13.60
```

Either of the other routes (2kg for £20, or twelve 100g bags for £21.60) might get one mark, but no more, as they are far more expensive than the example.

When you multiply, it can be difficult to decide where the decimal point belongs in the answer. You can use common sense (the example above is quite straightforward), or the following method:

5. (a)

	Has a Garden	Does Not Have a Garden
Interested in Moving House	10	20
Not Interested in Moving House	40	30

- Where the circles **overlap**, you can find the number of people who said **'yes' to both parts** of the survey.
- **Outside both circles** you can find the number who said **'no' to both**.
  - However, this number is missing – but we know that Ulrika interviewed 100 people in total. The numbers in the circles add up to 70, so the missing number ('?') must be 30.

(b) *Most people without a garden do not want to move house. However, they are still more likely than people who do have a garden to want to move house.*

To get two marks, you need to show some awareness of the ideas in **both parts of the example**.

- On the one hand, not having a garden doesn't make everybody desperate to move.
- On the other hand, it does seem to **increase** the number of people who want to change their home.

6.

There are two possible sets of answers to **Q 6 (b)-(d)**. From the two centimetre grids which follow, choose the one which more closely matches yours.

(a) (See below)

Remember that the **first** number of (**a** , **b**) tells you **how far to count across** in the *x* direction, and the **second** tells you **how far up** towards *y*.

- Two marks for three correct coordinates.

- One mark for e.g. one wrong, or mixing up the *x* and *y* directions.

If your answers to (**a**) and to (**b**) (**i**) contain mistakes, you can still get the marks in later sections if you move and measure your shape effectively.

Option 1:

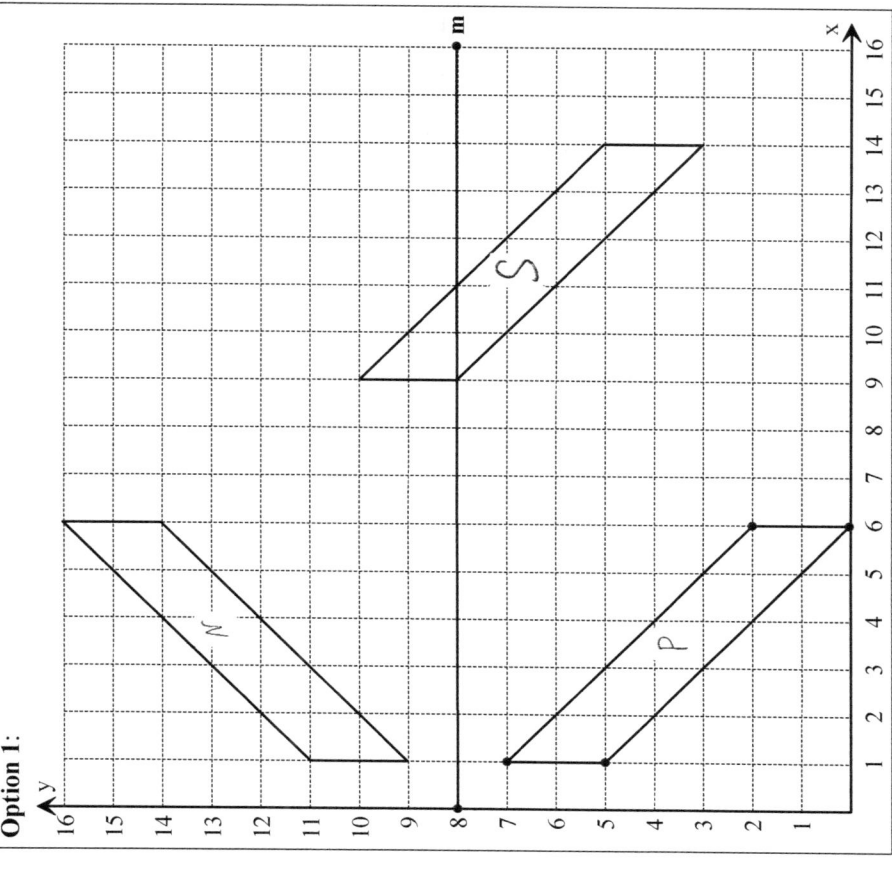

Option 2:

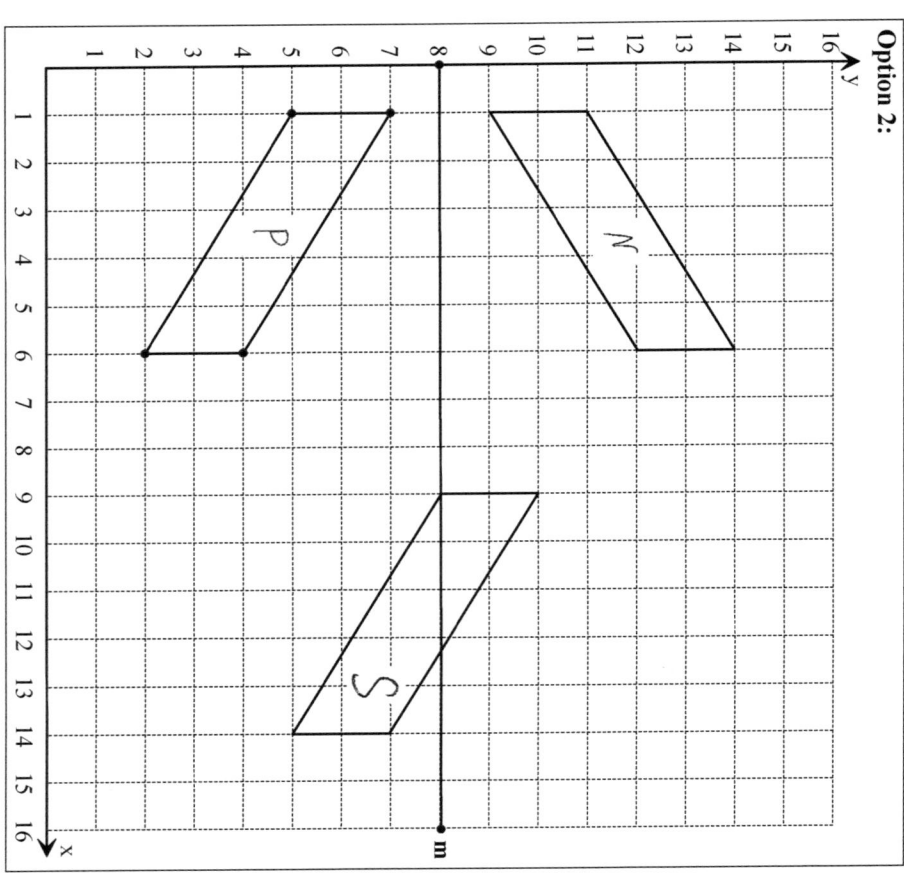

(b) **(i)** (See above)

Remember that a **parallelogram** has **two pairs of parallel sides**, which are **not all the same length**. It is as though you have taken a rectangle and squeezed the diagonally opposite corners towards each other.

You might lose half a mark if you forget to label your shape.

(ii) (6, 4) or (6, 0)

- One mark if one number is right, or if they are both right but the wrong way round.

(iii) 2

Rotational symmetry is **how many times a shape fits into its original 'footprint' in a complete 360° rotation**. A parallelogram does so twice (after half a turn and when it returns to the starting point), so it has an order of rotational symmetry of 2.

- 1 is the lowest order of rotational symmetry.

(c) (See above)

(d) (See above)

(e) 10 cm^2

You can find the area in one of two ways:

- Look at the squares within the shape, counting each part square with another that combines with it to make a whole:

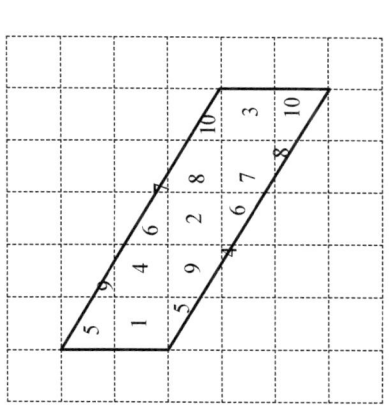

- Multiply the height of a short side by the total horizontal width, so that $2 \times 5 = 10$ in the diagram here:

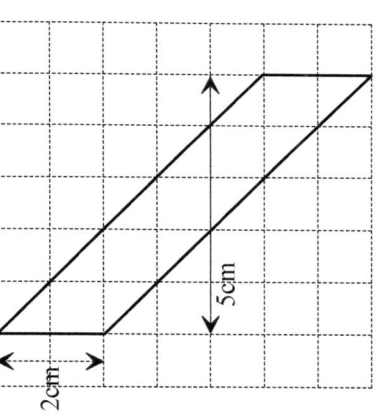

7. (a)

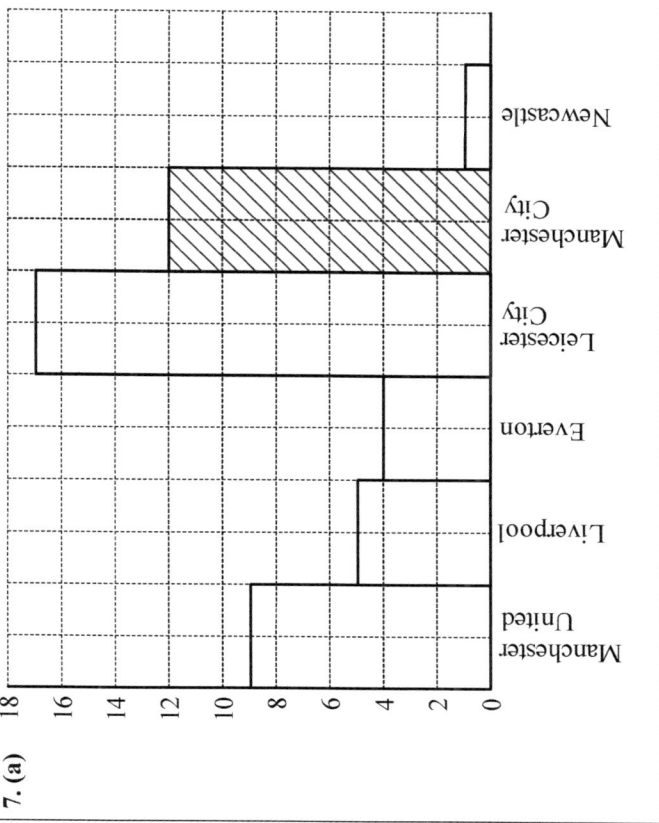

- Take away a mark for each error or significant inaccuracy.

(b) (i) $17 - 1 = 16$

The **range** is the difference between the largest and smallest number in the data set.

(ii)

$9 + 5 + 4 + 17 + 12 + 1$
$= 14 + 21 + 13$
$= 48$

$6 \overline{)48}$ = 8

8 supporters

See **Q 3 (c)** if you need to revise the concept of a **mean**.

(iii)

1	4	5	9	12	17
X	4	5	9	12	~~17~~
X	~~4~~	⑤	~~9~~	~~12~~	~~17~~

$\frac{5+9}{2} = \frac{14}{2} = 7$ supporters

The **median** is another sort of average. To find it:

- Put the data (numbers) in order from **smallest to largest**.
- Find the **middle number or numbers** by crossing out the end numbers in pairs.
- If you have **one number**, this is the median.
- If you have **two numbers**, you must **find their mean** (add them and halve the result); or to put it another way, you must go **half way between them**.

(c)

$$\underline{\underline{8}}$$

If the mean does not change when you add another number, this number **must be the same as the mean**:

$$\frac{48}{6} \qquad \frac{48 + 8}{7} = 8$$

- There are two marks for this because the concept requires some thought – not because you need to show working.

---

8. (a) (i)

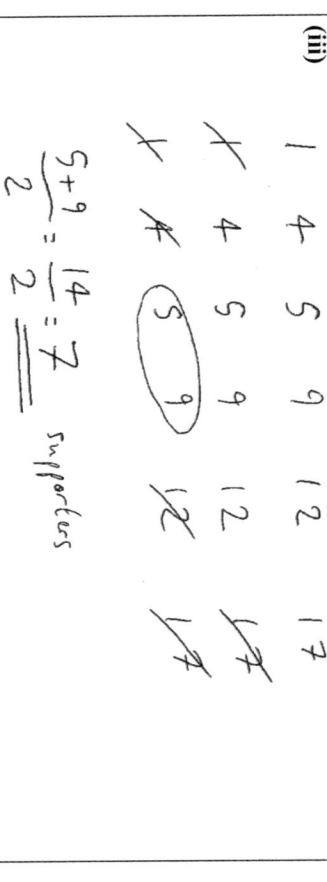

'Of' means 'multiply'.

Notice the cancelling: 5 goes into 5 once and into 900 180 times.

- Alternatively, **divide 900 by 5** (which gives 180), then **multiply the answer by 2**.

900 can be written as $\frac{900}{1}$.

(ii)

$\frac{2}{5} = \frac{40}{100} = 40\%$ $100\% - 40\% = \underline{\underline{60\%}}$

How much is **left**?

(b) **Method 1**: Finding a percentage by using **decimals** (my favourite method)

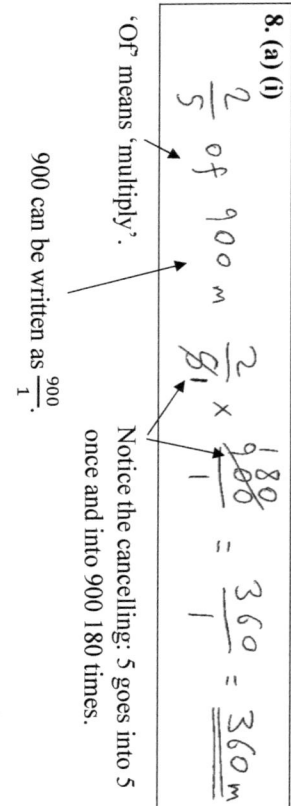

Remember that 'of' means 'multiply'.

For a discussion of multiplication and decimals, see **Q 4 (a) (i)**. I like this method because it is effective even for very fiddly numbers.

- For instance, what is 36.7% of 83? No problem: just multiply 0.367 by 83 using the column method, as in the example (the answer is 30.461, by the way).

Method 2: Finding a percentage by using fractions

15% of 900 m

$15\% = \dfrac{15}{100} \cdot 900 = \dfrac{900}{1}$

$\dfrac{15}{100} \times \dfrac{900}{1} = 135\,m$

Because $\dfrac{135}{1} = 135$.

'Percent' literally means 'out of' (*per*) '100' (*cent*).

Be aware that <u>diagonal cancelling only works for multiplication</u>: **do not** use it when dividing, adding or subtracting fractions (you can still cancel the top and bottom of the same fraction, though).

9.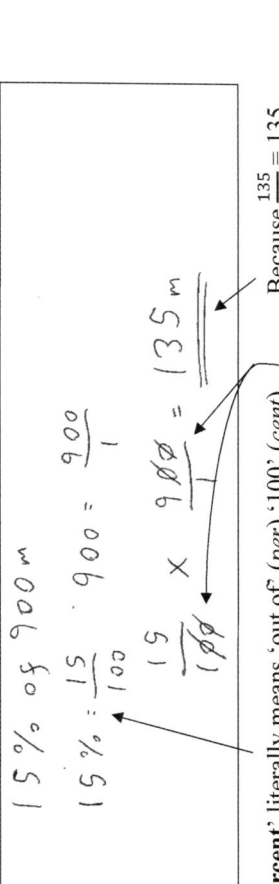

$\dfrac{1}{2}$ is largest — Using **common sense**!

$\dfrac{3}{8}$ must be larger than $\dfrac{3}{10}$ — Because if you divide a pizza into 8 slices, each slice is bigger than if you had cut it into 10.

Finding a **common denominator**

$\dfrac{2}{5} = \dfrac{6}{15}$, $\dfrac{1}{3} = \dfrac{5}{15}$, $\dfrac{4 \cdot 5}{15}$

$\dfrac{1}{2}$ (But what about $\dfrac{3}{8}$?)

$\dfrac{2}{5}$ so $\dfrac{3}{8}$ is larger.

$\dfrac{3}{10}$

$\dfrac{1}{3} = \dfrac{3}{9}$ so $\dfrac{3}{8}$ is larger.

$\dfrac{2}{5} = \dfrac{16}{40}$, $\dfrac{3}{8} = \dfrac{15}{40}$ so $\dfrac{2}{5}$ is larger.

So $\dfrac{3}{8}$ goes

$\dfrac{3}{10}, \dfrac{1}{3}, \dfrac{3}{8}, \dfrac{2}{5}, \dfrac{1}{2}$

You do not need to write as much working as in the example! I have included every small step, for clarity. The same goes for many of the answers in this pack.

10. (a) Method 1: Flow Chart

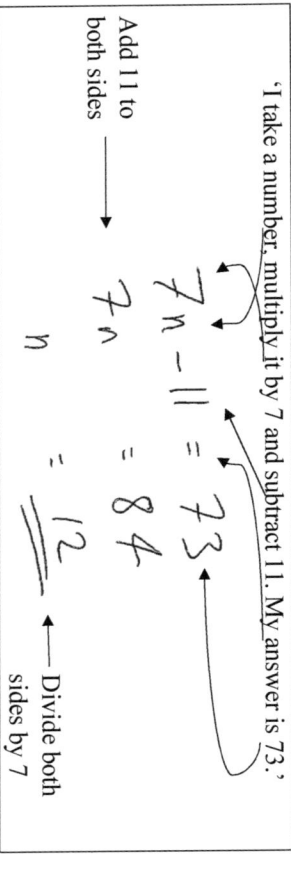

This is probably the most straightforward method for solving this question. See how the direction is reversed, and so are the operations (× becomes ÷, − becomes +).

In this, and the other methods below, the unknown number is called 'n' for simplicity.

Method 2: Algebra

'I take a number, multiply it by 7 and subtract 11. My answer is 73.'

Your first target with an equation like this is to have all the letters (here '7n') by themselves on one side of the '=' sign. To do this you need to remove the −11 by adding 11 to both sides.

- '7n' is a way of writing '7 × n' or 'n × 7'.

- Add 11 to both sides → $7n - 11 = 73$
  $7n = 84$

- Divide both sides by 7 → $n = \underline{\underline{12}}$

Method 3: Trial and Improvement

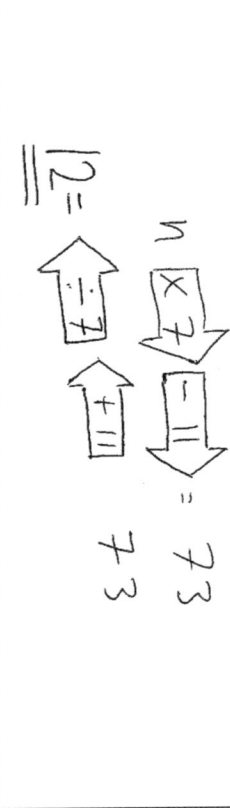

This method involves trying out different values for the number you are seeking, getting closer and closer to the answer – zooming in, if you like.

(b) Method 1: Algebra

$$\left(\frac{n}{5}\right)^2 = 64$$

- Square root ('un-square') both sides → $\frac{n}{5} = 8$

- Multiply both sides by 5 → $n = 8 \times 5 = \underline{\underline{40}}$

However, it is possible to get through the majority of 11+ exams without knowing algebra, for example by using a method such as the following:

Method 2: Trial and Improvement

$$(? - 5) \times (? - 5) = 64$$

$? = 20: (20 \div 5) \times (20 \div 5) = 4 \times 4 = 16$ too low
$? = 50: (50 \div 5) \times (50 \div 5) = 10 \times 10 = 100$ too high
$? = 40: (40 \div 5) \times (40 \div 5) = 8 \times 8 = 64$ ✓

40

You keep going until you get the answer (or, if the answer is a decimal, until you are close enough).

When you use trial and improvement, **avoid trying consecutive numbers** (20, 21, 22, 23, 24, 25 …). This way you will spend the whole exam on one question! Be prepared to make big leaps, such as 20, 50, 40 in the example.

(c) **23**

If you are unsure about primes or factors, see **Qs 1 & 3**.

(d) Method 1: Algebra

$$\frac{6n - 12}{2} = 2n$$

$6n - 12 = 4n$
$6n - 4n = 12$
$2n = 12$
$n = 6$

Method 2: Trial and Improvement

$$(? \times 6 - 12) \div 2 = 2 \times ?$$

$? = 10: (10 \times 6 - 12) \div 2 = 48$ $48 \neq 2 \times 10$ too high
$? = 5: (5 \times 6 - 12) \div 2 = 9$ $9 \neq 2 \times 5$ too low
$? = 7: (7 \times 6 - 12) \div 2 = 15$ $15 \neq 2 \times 7$ too high
$? = 6: (6 \times 6 - 12) \div 2 = 12$ $12 = 2 \times 6$ ✓

'not equal to'

6

11.

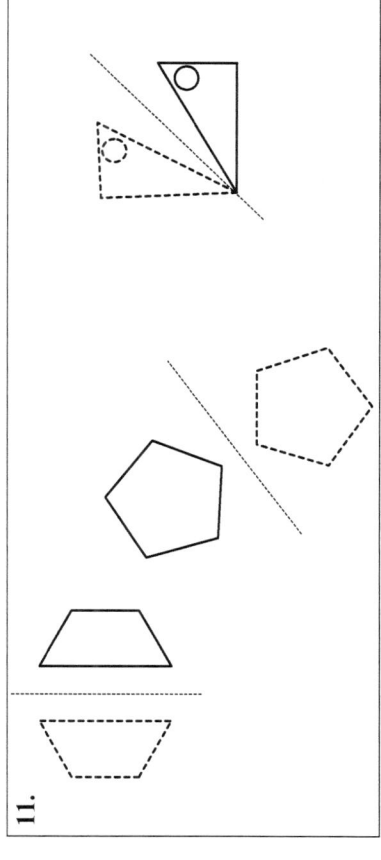

Your answers do not need to be millimetre-perfect, but you will lose marks for significant inaccuracy.

- Be sure to reflect each point/corner straight across the mirror line, by the shortest route.
- Check that each point is the same distance from the mirror line as its reflection.

12. (a) (i) $17\tfrac{1}{2}$ hours   **or**   17 hrs 30 mins

Anything **between** (but not equal to) **17 hours** and **18 hours** should be fine. An answer of exactly 17 or 18 would probably lose a mark.

(ii) £390

(b) (i) (See above)

(ii)

Because the distance on the map is 3.5 cm, whereas the scale is in 2 cm units (an increase of 175%, or × $1\frac{3}{4}$ (1.75), the 1 km distance in the scale must be increased by the same amount. 1 × 1.75 = 1.75, so the real-life distance is 1.75 km.

Don't forget that (to the nearest 0.5 km) **1.75 rounds UP to 2**, not down to 1.5. (You will lose a mark if you get this wrong.)

Here is another way of thinking about it:

2 cm : 1 km
therefore 1 cm : 0.5 km / 500 m

3.5 cm : 1.75 km

The method is very similar, but it involves **reducing the scale to 1 cm increments**, and building up to 3.5 from there.

(iii)

time = $\frac{distance}{speed}$ = $\frac{2}{1.5}$ = $\frac{4}{3}$ = $1\frac{1}{3}$ hours = 1 hr 20 mins

Be very careful when converting fractions or decimals into times involving minutes or seconds: there are 60, not 100 minutes in an hour (and seconds in a minute).

Anything **between £380 and £395** ought to be safe.

(b) They did not, because the minimum charge to rent from Neardeath is £150.

Or

(b) They did not, because 2 hours with Neardeath costs nearly £200.

13. (a) (See above)

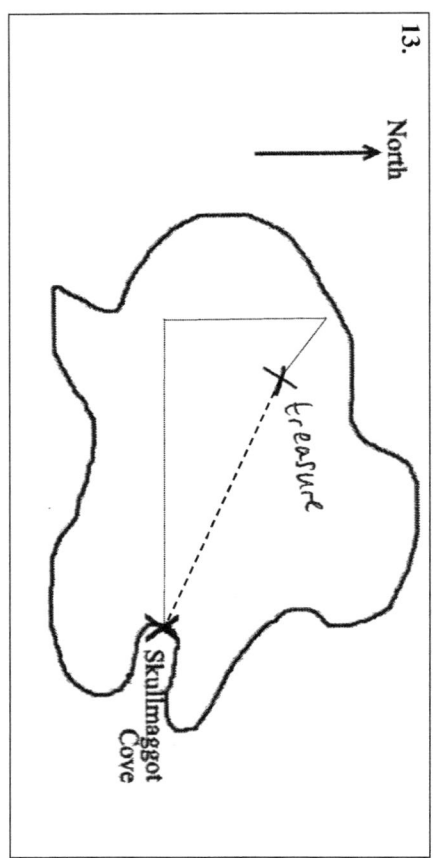

A scale of **2 cm : 1 km** means that 2 km should be drawn as 4 cm, and 1 km as 2 cm, and 500 m as 1 cm.

- For this and for the questions below, drawing inaccuracy **up to 1 or 2 mm** is likely to be tolerated. For example, the short line in the example, running SE towards the treasure, may in fact be a little north of SE.

- Furthermore, answers based on an inaccurate response to a previous part of the question **should still be given credit** if they are correct on their own terms (follow-through marking).

Lengths in the example answer may be slightly inaccurate, owing to printing adjustments.

- For example, 0.5 hours **is not 50 minutes**!

If you got an answer other than 2 for part (ii), but used it correctly here, you should still get the marks.

For all calculations involving speed, the '**SDT Triangle**' is very useful:

Cover the value you are looking for to discover the necessary operation involving the other 2 values.

In the question we are looking for **time**, so we cover this and see $\frac{distance}{speed}$. Therefore $time = \frac{distance}{speed}$.

Using the same method,
- $speed = \frac{distance}{time}$
- $distance = speed \times time$

[SDT Triangle: Distance on top, Speed and Time on bottom; divide, multiply]

14.

$14 - 1 = 13$
$123 + 13 = 136$

There must be the same number of pages after page 123 as before page 14.

15.

4	11	6
9	7	5
8	3	10

- Because every horizontal, vertical or diagonal which crosses the middle square shares that square's value, we can ignore that square for the moment. $10 + 4 = 14$ and $11 + 3 = 14$, so **the empty corner squares (top right and bottom left) must also add up to 14.**

- $11 + 4 = 15$ and $10 + 3 = 13$, so **the top right square must contain a number which is 2 smaller than the bottom left.**
  - Taking these two facts together, the top right number must be 6 and the bottom left must be 8.

Now we know that **each row, column or diagonal must add up to 21**, so it is easy to complete the rest of the square.

END

Paper 2: *Wei Wei's Pies*
Standard Level

1. I have these notes and coins in my pocket:

(a) From the numbers on the coins and notes above, write down:

(i) two factors of 12

Answer: …….. …..…. **(2)**

(ii) a multiple of 25

Answer: ……………… **(1)**

(iii) two different prime numbers

Answer: …….. …..…. **(2)**

(iv) three numbers with a product of 100

Answer: ….. ….. ….. **(1)**

(v) two numbers with a difference of 9

Answer: …….. …..…. **(1)**

(vi) a square number

Answer: ……………… **(1)**

(b) Which notes and coins should I use to pay exactly £38.58, leaving the greatest possible number of notes and coins in my pocket afterwards?

Answer: .... **(2)**

(c) If I paid £38.58 with the £50 note, how much change would I receive?

Answer: .... **(2)**

---

2. **(a)** Complete the following number patterns by filling in the gaps.

    (i)   4   12   20   28   ___

    (ii)   16   14   10   4   –4   ___

    (iii)   9   ___   25   ___   49

    (iv)   1   10   3   8   5   6   ___   ___   **(6)**

(b) Continue the following number patterns by applying the given rule.

    (i) Subtract 7 each time:

    31   ___   ___   ___   **(2)**

    (ii) Each number is the sum of all the previous numbers:

    1   ___   ___   ___   ___   **(2)**

    (iii) Find each number by subtracting 2 from the previous number, then doubling the result:

    5   ___   ___   ___   ___   **(2)**

3. This pictogram shows how many bananas the students in form 5B at Gobbly Grove Primary eat at lunchtime each day:

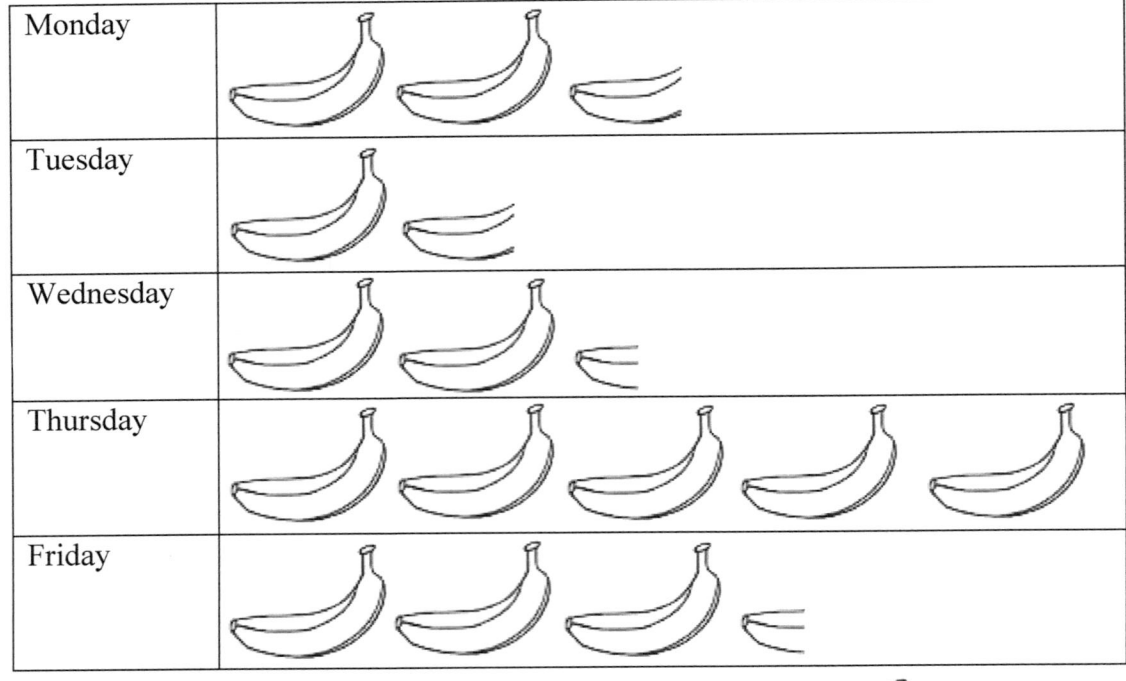

= 3 bananas

(a) How many bananas are eaten on

(i) Thursday? Answer: .... (1)

(ii) Friday? Answer: .... (1)

(b) What total number of bananas is eaten by 5B during the week?

Answer: .... (2)

(c) Louis says that Monday is the day when 5B eat the median number of bananas. Jade thinks he should have said 'mean' instead of 'median', but cannot say so because she is eating a banana.

Which of them is right – or are they both right?

Show your working.

Answer: .... (4)

4. **(a)** Draw all the lines of symmetry on the following shape:

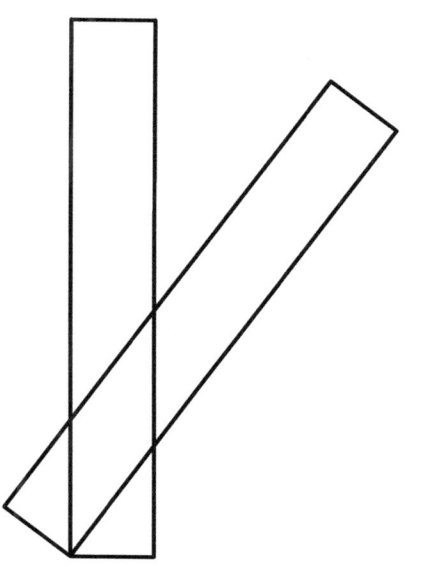

(2)

(b) Write down the order of rotational symmetry of each of the following shapes:

(i)	(ii)	(iii)	(iv)
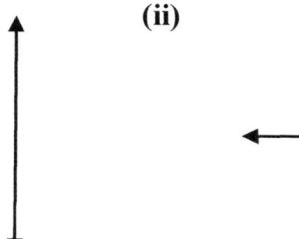	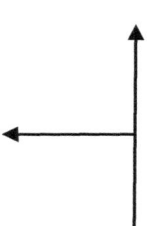	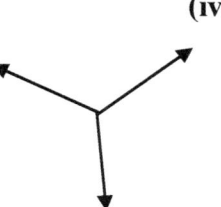	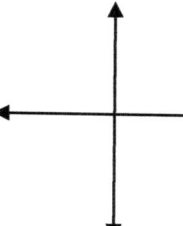
Answer:	Answer:	Answer:	Answer: .... (4)

5. Rank the following events using the letters, A, B, C and D, from most likely (A) to least likely (D):

- The world does not end tomorrow.   Rank: ......

- I throw 2 standard dice and the total is a prime number.   Rank: ......

- I flip a fair coin ten times and get heads every time.   Rank: ......

- A friend wins £1,000,000 in the lottery next week.   Rank: ......   (2)

6.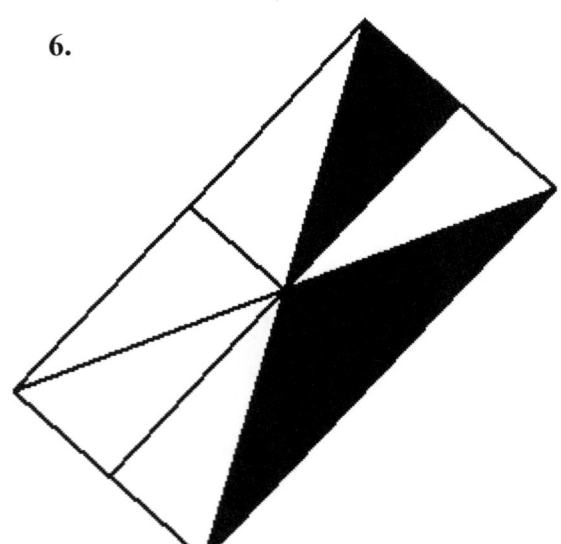

(a) What fraction of the rectangle has been shaded?

Answer: .... (1)

(b) Shade a further $\frac{1}{4}$ of the rectangle. (1)

(c) What fraction of the rectangle has now been shaded?

Answer: .... (2)

7. By shading the smallest possible number of squares, make this pattern symmetrical around the diagonal mirror line:

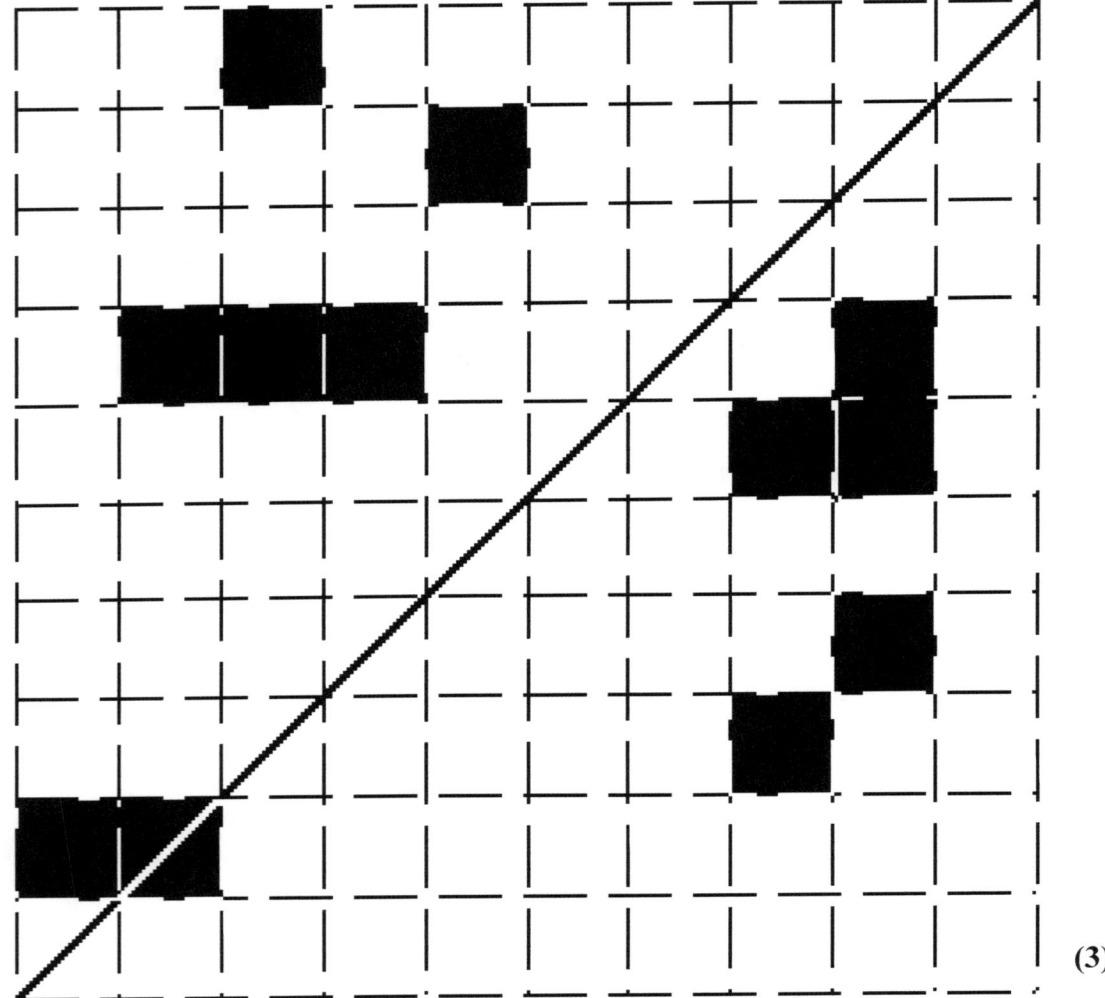

(3)

8. There are 12 people in Wei Wei's office. She feels bored and decides to ask all of them about their favourite pies. In order to avoid her work, she records their answers in the following chart:

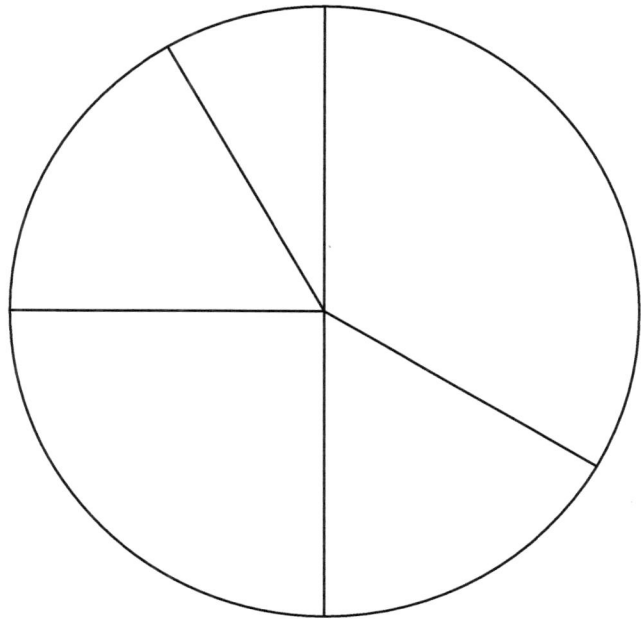

(a) Based on the following information, correctly label each section of the pie chart:

- 25% of the class like shepherd's pies.
- More people like pumpkin pies than say, 'I'm not interested in pies. Stop wasting time and do your work!'
- The same number of people like pumpkin pies and Cornish pasties.
- 4 people like fruit pies.

(4)

(b) Complete the following frequency table:

Favourite Pie	Frequency
Fruit Pie	
Cornish Pastie	
Shepherd's Pie	
Pumpkin Pie	
'I'm not interested in pies. Stop wasting time and do your work!'	

(2)

9. I find this mysterious solid object in the back of a drawer:

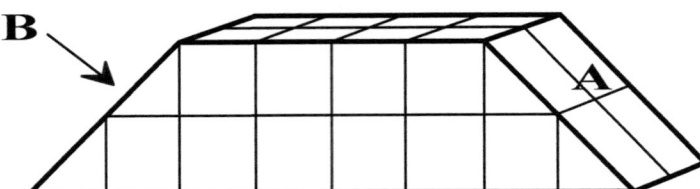

I paint the ends, A and B, with red nail polish. I paint the rest blue and draw a centimetre grid on the outside of the object.

(a) What is the total surface area painted blue?

Answer: .... (3)

(b) What is the volume of the object?

Answer: .... (3)

(c) On the grid below, draw a net which could be folded to make the object above. Two faces have been drawn for you:

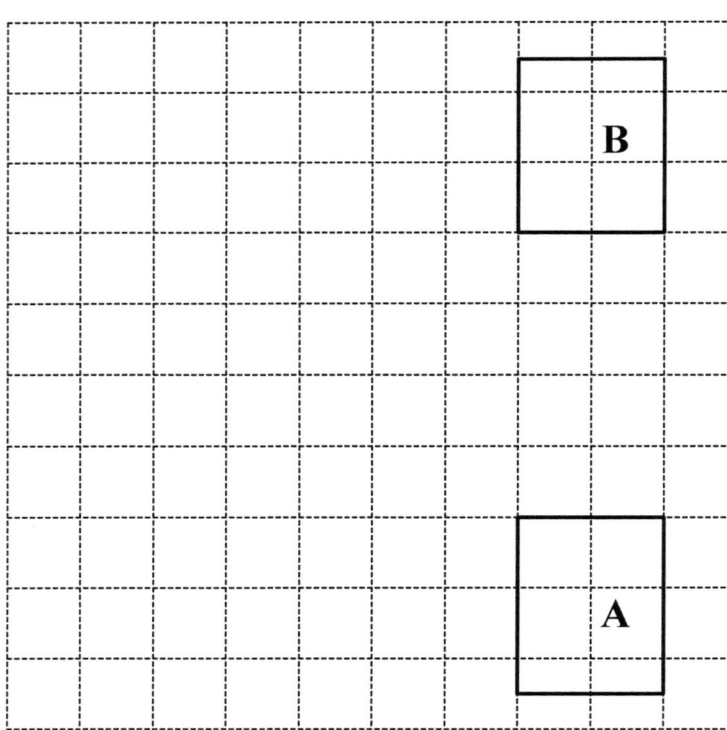

(3)

10. Write down the measurement shown on each of the following scales:

(a)

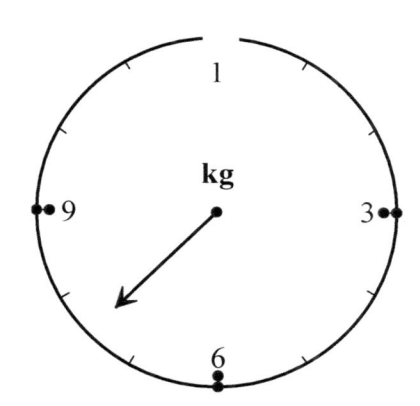

(b)

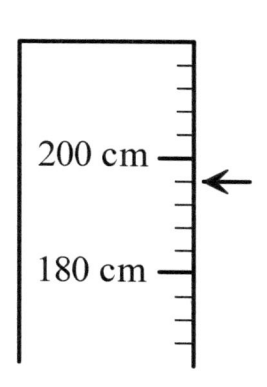

Answer: ....   Answer: ....   **(4)**

11. (a) On the centimetre grid below, plot the points (3 , 2), (4 , 6) and (9 , 2) and join them to form a triangle. Label your triangle **T**. **(2)**

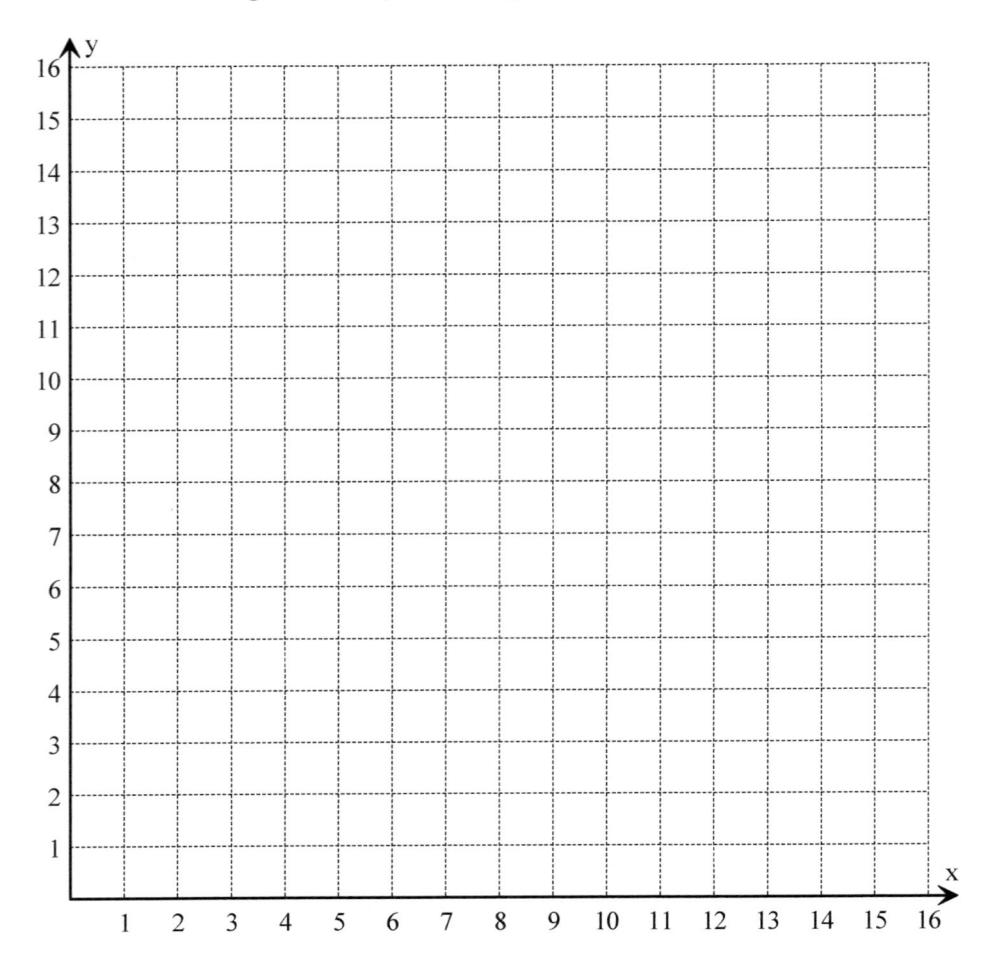

(b) What is the area of triangle **T**?

Answer: ……………… **(2)**

(c) Rotate the triangle 90° clockwise about the point (10 , 1). Label the new triangle **Q**. **(3)**

(d) Translate triangle **Q** 6 squares in the *y* direction and –7 squares in the *x* direction. Label the new triangle **P**. **(2)**

12. Draw a line to match each of the items on the left to the most appropriate units on the right. (Two units will be left over.)

	ml
The amount of lemonade in a glass	kg
The length of a motor race	km
The amount of rock in the Earth	mm
The length of an ant	km³
The mass (weight) of a baby	g
	l

(5)

13. **(a)** Draw the given times on the clock faces below.

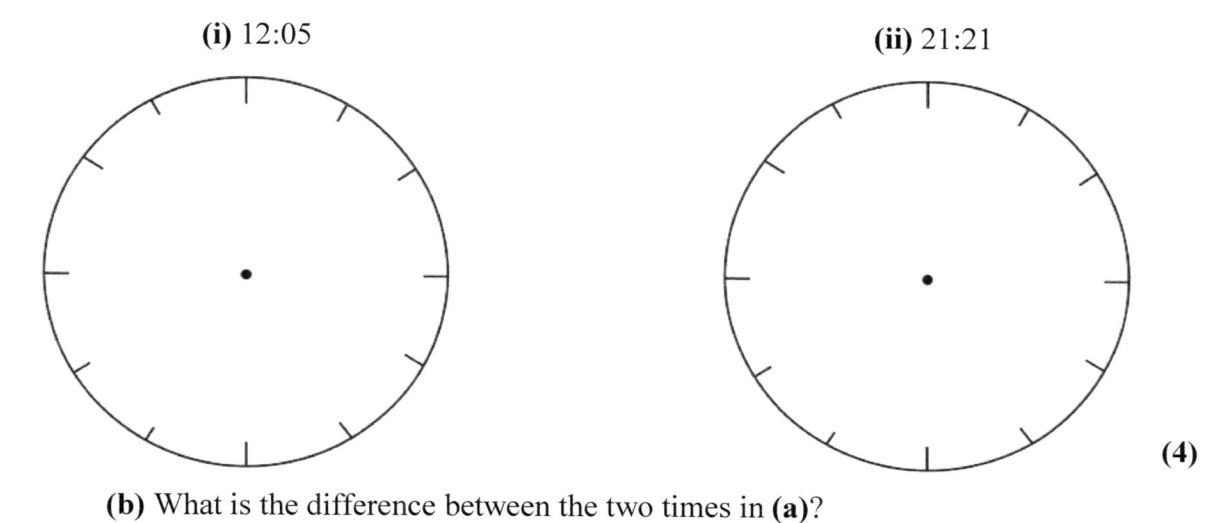

(i) 12:05

(ii) 21:21

(4)

(b) What is the difference between the two times in **(a)**?

……. hrs ……. mins **(2)**

14. There are 5 squares in this picture:

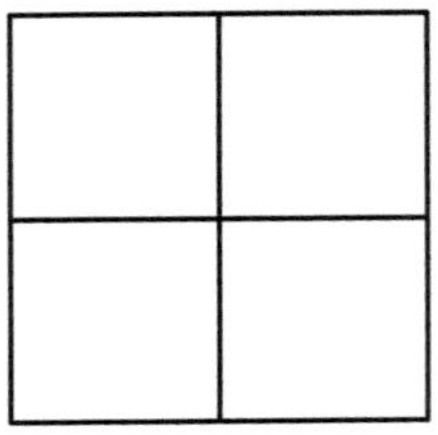

    How many rectangles and squares are in the following picture?

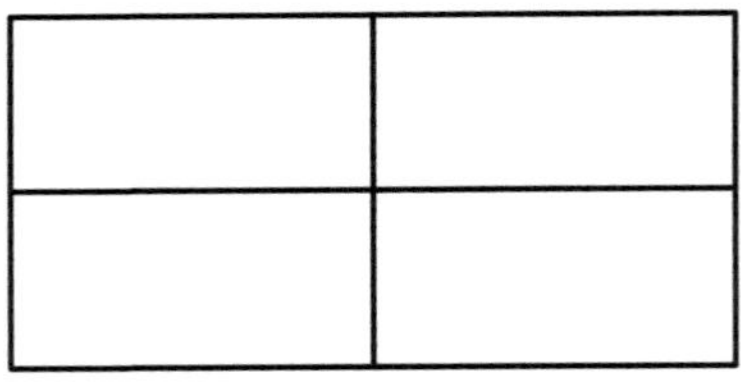

    Answer: ……………… (3)

---

15. The length of this rectangle is 3 times its width:

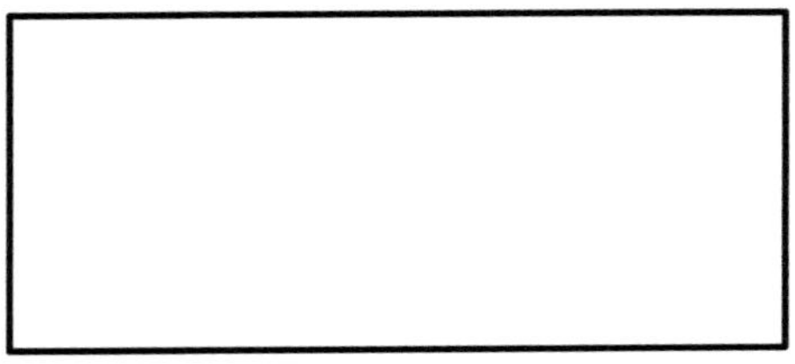

    (Not to scale)

    Its area is 192 cm².

    What is its perimeter?

    Answer: ……………… (4)

16. Write down 5 numbers which have:
- a median of 3
- a mode of 2
- a mean of 6
- a range of 12

Answer: …… …… …… …… …… (3)

17. (a) What is 32% of 150?

Answer: ……………… (2)

(b) Wig Wam Wig Emporium is running the following promotion:

15% Off All Wigs!

Donald bought his wig for £85 before this special offer began. What would it have cost to buy it now?

Answer: ……………… (2)

TOTAL MARKS: 100

Paper 2: Wei Wei's Pies

Solutions

1. (a) (i) For an explanation of **factors**, see **Paper 1, Q1(d)**.

$$\underline{\underline{1 \quad 2}}$$

(ii) $25 \times 2 = 50 \quad \underline{\underline{50}}$

(iii) For **multiples**, see **Paper 1, Q3(a)(ii)**.

$$\underline{\underline{2 \quad 5}}$$

(iv) For **prime numbers**, see **Paper 1, Q3(a)(i)**.

1 , 50 , 2 or 1 , 20 , 5

or 1 , 10 , 10 or 2 , 5 , 10

(v) You need three numbers which **multiply** to make 100.

$$\underline{\underline{1, 10}} \qquad 10 - 1 = 9$$

(vi) You find the **difference** between two numbers by **subtracting the smaller from the larger**.

$$\underline{\underline{1}} \qquad 1^2 = 1 \times 1 = 1$$

(b) A **square number** is a number which is **made by multiplying a number by itself**. It is easy to miss the fact that 1 is a square number.

£20, £10, £5, £2, £1, 50p, 5p, 2p, 1p

(c) A combination which does add up correctly, but which uses more than 9 pieces of money, would get one mark.

$$\begin{array}{r} {}^{4}\cancel{5}\cancel{0}.\cancel{0}\cancel{0} \\ -38.58 \\ \hline 11.42 \end{array} \qquad \underline{\underline{£11.42}}$$

If you get a wrong answer because of a slight error (while using essentially the correct method), you should receive one mark.

2. (a) (i) The method of writing differences is very, very useful when answering sequence questions.

4 $\overset{+8}{\frown}$ 12 $\overset{+8}{\frown}$ 20 $\overset{+8}{\frown}$ 28 $\overset{+8}{\frown}$ ㊱

(ii) This is an example of how the difference method makes an apparently complex sequence problem easy to solve.

16 $\overset{-2}{\frown}$ 14 $\overset{-4}{\frown}$ 10 $\overset{-6}{\frown}$ 4 $\overset{-8}{\frown}$ -4 $\overset{-10}{\frown}$ ⊖14

(iii)

9 ⑯ 25 ㊱ 49

(3²) 4² (5²) 6² (7²)

When the difference method doesn't help and values in a sequence increase quite steeply, it is wise to look for square numbers.

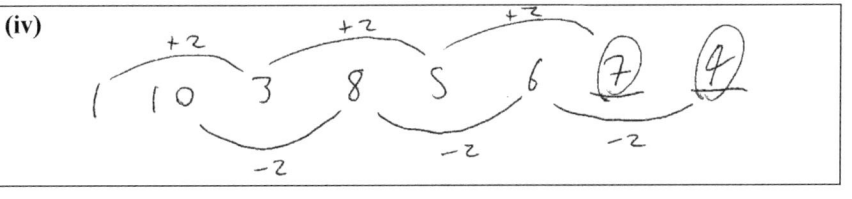

(iv)

10, 3, 8, 5, 6, 7, 4
(with +2, -5, +2, -2, -2, -2 differences shown; 7 and 4 circled)

And now for a really annoying one! If the numbers seem completely random, look carefully to see whether **two sequences are overlapping**. At 11+ there will not be more than two overlapping sequences, and each of them is likely to be very simple.

(b) (i)

31 24 17 10

This is quite simple, though it is a common mistake to write 26 rather than 24.

(ii)

1 1 2 4 8

Be sure to read the instructions carefully and accurately!

(iii)

5 6 8 12 20

---

3. (a) (i) 15   **(ii)** 10   **(iii)** 45

Pictogram questions are largely **a test of whether you can understand and use a key**: in this case, the key tells us that **1 banana image means 3 actual bananas**.

(c) Median: 8, 5, 7, 15, 10

8, 7, (8), 10, 15
          ↑
       Monday (Louis is right)

Mean: $\frac{\text{Total Bananas}}{\text{Number of Days}} = \frac{45}{5} = 9$ ← Not Monday (Jade is wrong)

Louis is right

For a discussion of the word **mean**, see **Paper 1, Q3(c)**. For the **median**, see **Paper 1, Q7(b)(iii)**.

---

4. (a)

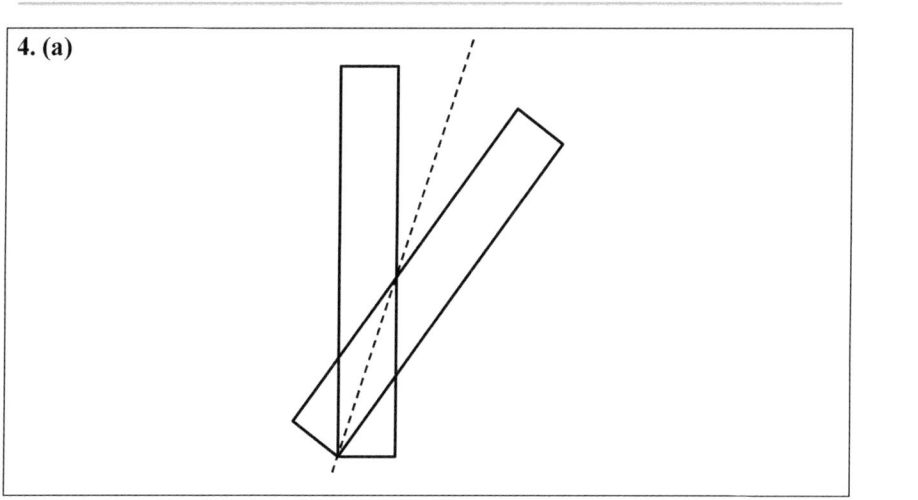

People sometimes find diagonal lines of symmetry difficult.

- Take time to find the best alignment of your ruler **before** you draw a line.

A broadly correct answer, but with an inaccurately drawn line, would get one mark.

For a discussion of **rotational symmetry**, see **Paper 1, Q6(b)(iii)**.

(b) (i) 2 (ii) 1 (iii) 3 (iv) 1

5.
- The world does not end tomorrow. Rank: A
- I throw 2 standard dice and the total is a prime number. Rank: B
- I flip a fair coin ten times and get heads every time. Rank: C
- A friend wins £1,000,000 in the lottery next week. Rank: D

It might be confusing that the options are in fact already in the correct order!

It is possible (indeed, best) to answer this question using common sense. However, it is possible to work out the answer using some maths:

- Here are the **15 ways of making prime numbers** with two dice:

  2: 1,1
  3: 1,2 2,1
  5: 1,4 2,3 3,2 4,1
  7: 1,6 2,5 3,4 4,3 5,2 6,1
  11: 6,5 5,6

  There are **a total of 36 combinations** which can be made with two dice (6×6).

  $\frac{15}{36} = \frac{5}{12}$ so **the probability of throwing two standard dice and getting a prime number is $\frac{5}{12}$**.

- It is very likely that the world does not end tomorrow.

- The chance of getting heads on **a single throw** is $\frac{1}{2}$. The chance of getting heads on **every one of 10 throws** is $\left(\frac{1}{2}\right)^{10}$ or $\frac{1}{2} \times \frac{1}{2} \times \frac{1}{2} \times \frac{1}{2} \times \frac{1}{2} \times \frac{1}{2} \times \frac{1}{2} \times \frac{1}{2} \times \frac{1}{2} \times \frac{1}{2} = \frac{1}{1024}$. This is very unlikely.

- However, winning a million pounds in the lottery is (sadly) far less likely.

6. (a) $\frac{3}{8}$

The triangle has been divided into 8 equal pieces, and 3 of these have been shaded.

(b) You need to have shaded any 2 more eighths (sections) of the shape.

This is because $\frac{1}{4} = \frac{2}{8}$.

(c) $\frac{5}{8}$

The easiest approach simply says that the triangle **was divided into 8** equal pieces, and **5 of them are now shaded in**.

Another approach, shown on the right in the example box, **adds a quarter to the $\frac{3}{8}$ which we started with**.

$\left(\frac{1}{4} + \frac{3}{8} = \frac{2}{8} + \frac{3}{8} = \frac{5}{8}\right)$

7.

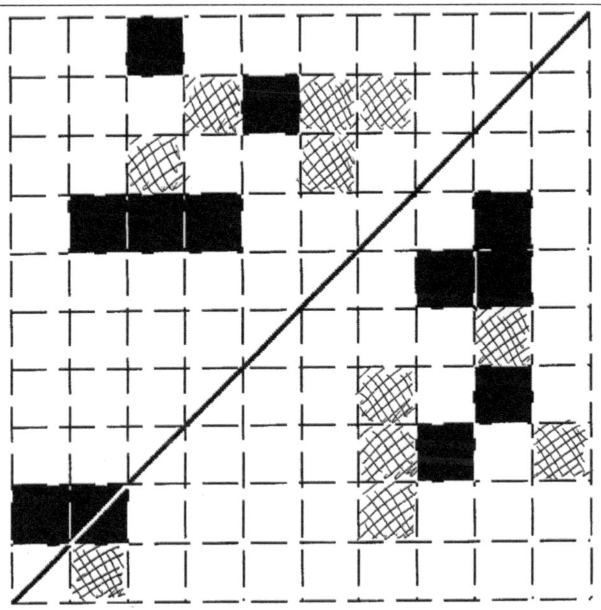

Work square by square.
- Count from a shaded square to the mirror line **by the shortest route.**
- Continue past the mirror line for **the same distance.**

- 2 marks for a minor error or two.
- 1 mark for several errors but some correct work.

8. (a)

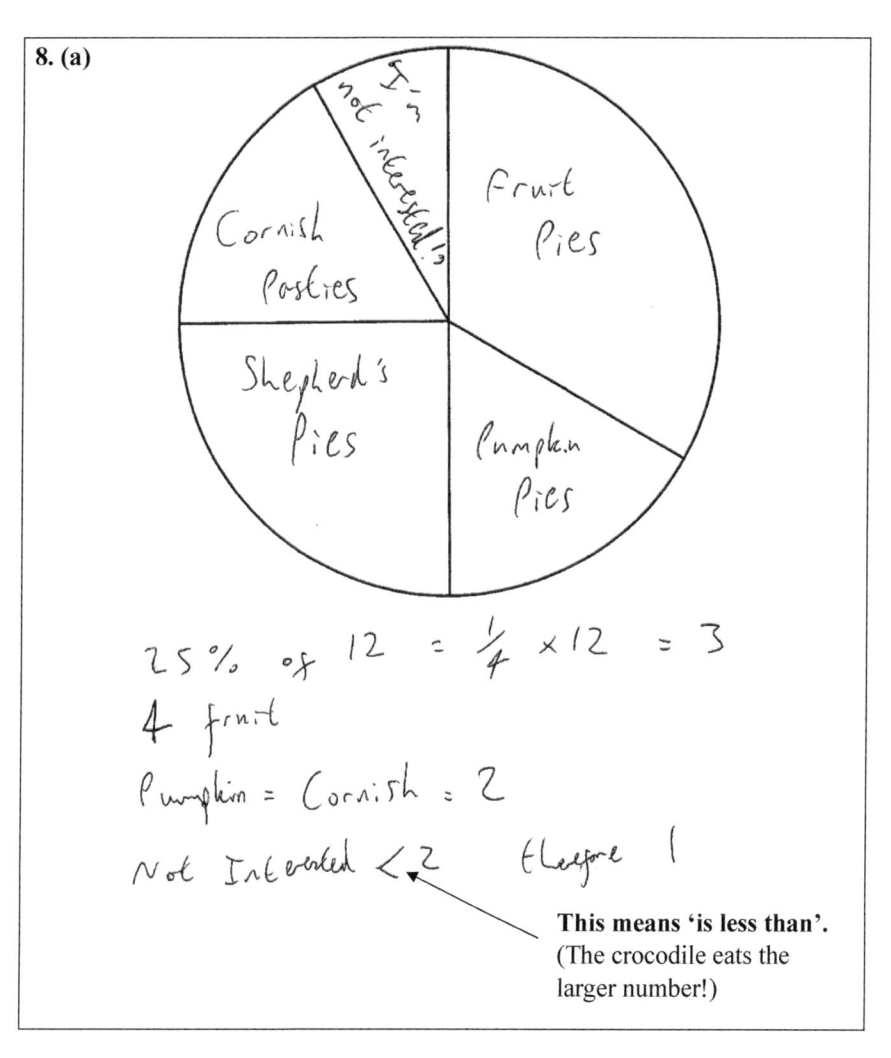

25% of 12 = ¼ × 12 = 3

4 fruit
Pumpkin = Cornish = 2
Not Interested < 2 therefore 1

This means 'is less than'. (The crocodile eats the larger number!)

(b)

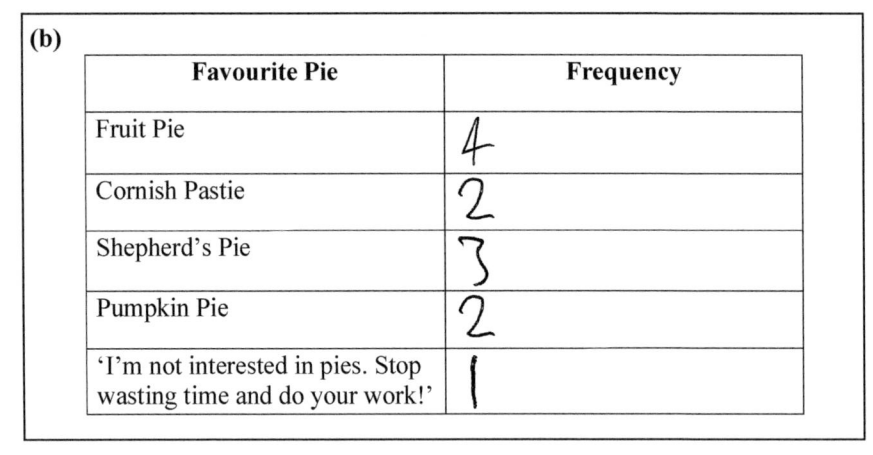

Favourite Pie	Frequency
Fruit Pie	4
Cornish Pastie	2
Shepherd's Pie	3
Pumpkin Pie	2
'I'm not interested in pies. Stop wasting time and do your work!'	1

9. (a)

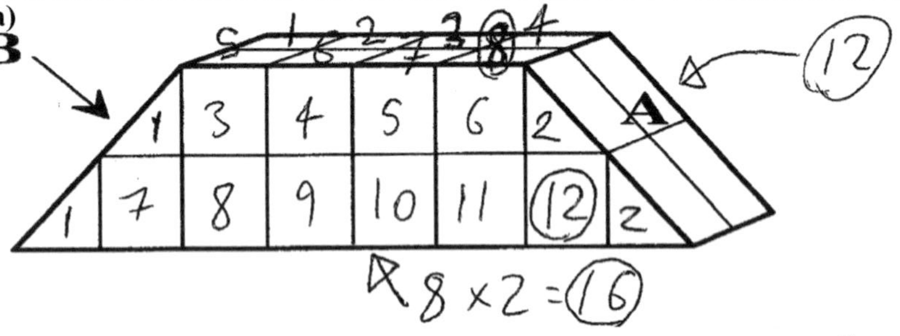

The simplest approach is to count squares.

- 2 half squares make 1 square.
- You must work out the areas of the two **hidden sides**.

Be very careful to write the **correct units**.

$$12 + 12 + 8 + 16 = \underline{48 \text{ cm}^2}$$

8 × 2 = 16

(b)

$$12 \times 2 = \underline{24 \text{ cm}^3}$$

This object has one face (the side nearest to us) whose shape continues all the way through to the back (this means that this solid is called a **prism**).

Therefore you must take **the area of the front** (12 cm²) and **multiply it by the depth** (2cm).

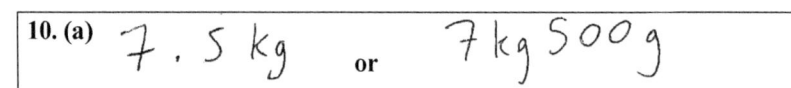

(c)

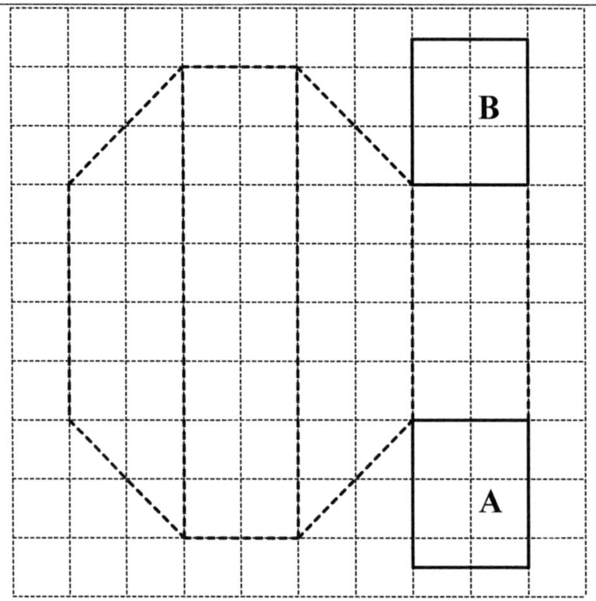

10. (a) 7.5 kg or 7 kg 500 g

It is a very good idea to **write in some of the missing numbers** before answering a question of this sort.

(b) 196 cm

This is slightly trickier. The difference between 180 and 200 is 20, and there are 5 gaps. 20 ÷ 5 = 4, so **each gap is worth 4 cm**.

11.

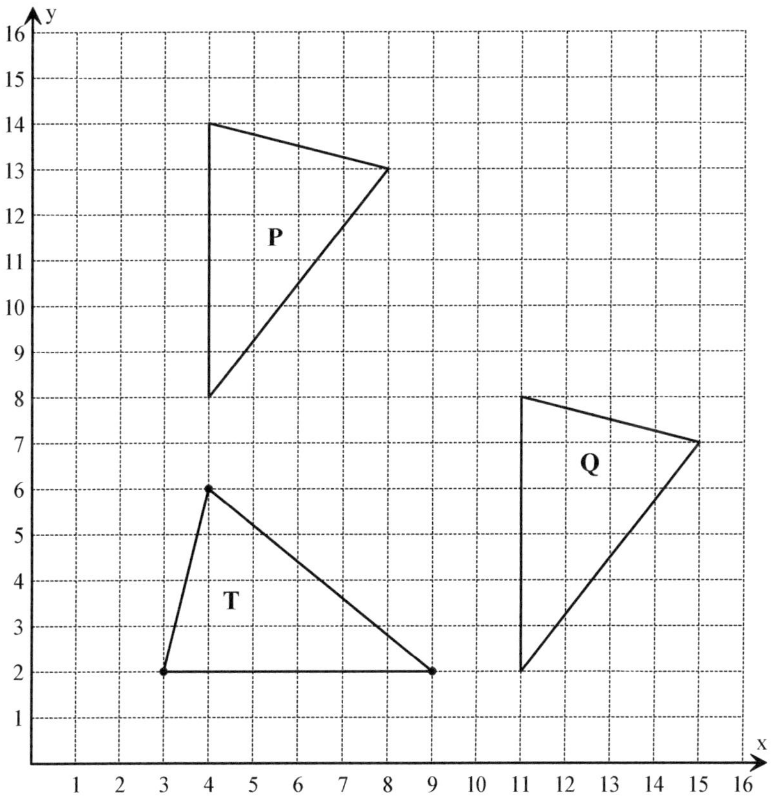

[Grid showing triangles P, Q, and T on coordinate axes from 0 to 16 on x-axis and 0 to 16 on y-axis]

(b) $\dfrac{6 \times 4}{2} = 12 \text{ cm}^2$

The area of a triangle is found by **multiplying the length of the base by the perpendicular height and dividing by 2.**

$$area = \dfrac{base \times height}{2}$$

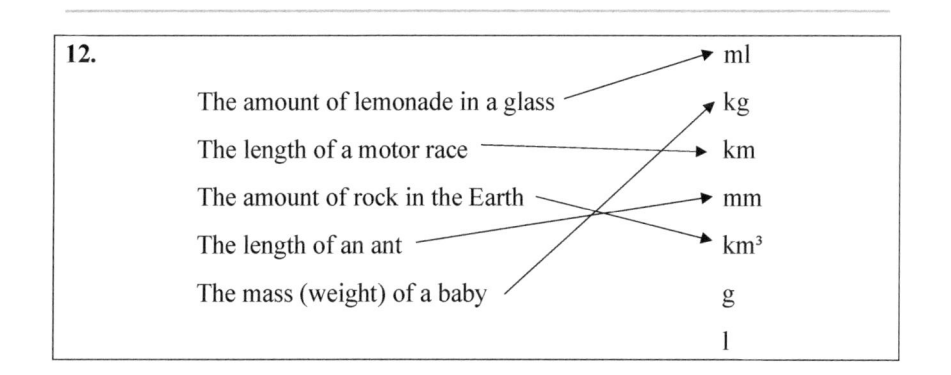

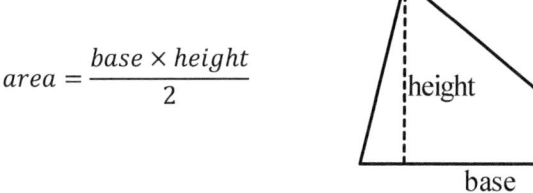

(c) Imagine that the point (10, 1) is at the centre of a wheel, and triangle T is drawn on the wheel. Imagine turning the wheel 90° (a quarter turn) to the right (clockwise).

For an accurate answer, **do this point by point**. Make sure that each point **remains the same distance from (10, 1).**

(d) Translate means 'move'.

12.

The amount of lemonade in a glass → ml
The length of a motor race → kg
The amount of rock in the Earth → km
The length of an ant → mm
The mass (weight) of a baby → km³
→ g
→ l

13.

(i) 12:05   **(ii)** 21:21

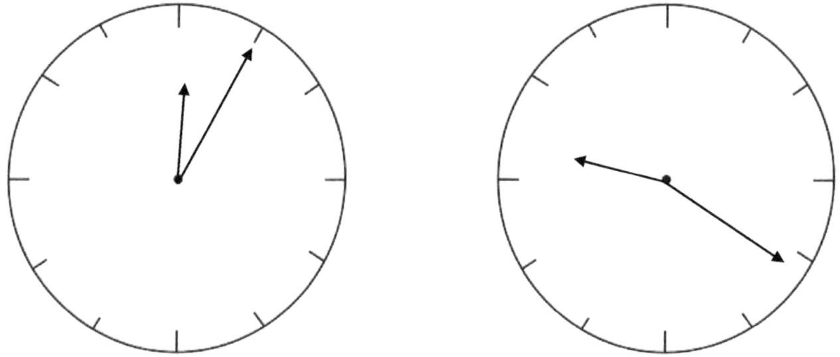

The **minute hand** needs to be **accurate.**

The **hour hand** needs to be **reasonably accurate**. For **(i)**, you *might* get away with an hour hand pointing straight at 12, but for **(ii)** the hour hand needs to be about $\frac{1}{3}$ of the way between 9 and 10.

- If you are unhappy when working with the 24 hour clock, remember that **6pm is 18:00**, and count from there.

(b)

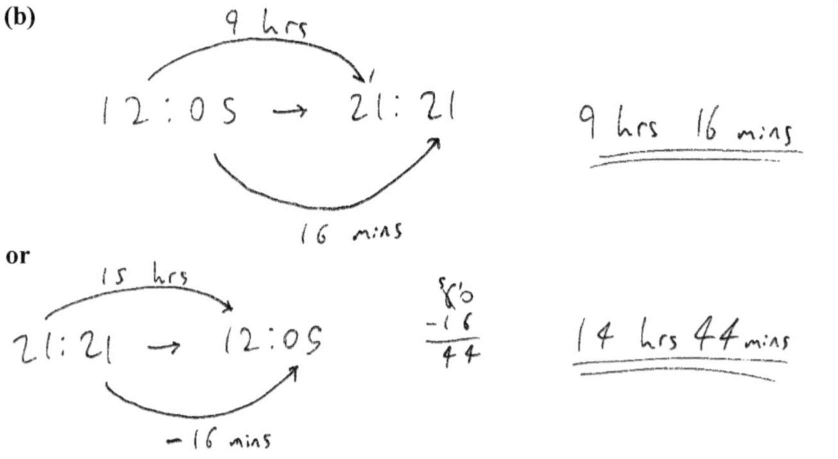

12:05 → 21:21   9 hrs

12:05 → 21:21   16 mins

9 hrs 16 mins

or

21:21 → 12:05   15 hrs

21:21 → 12:05   -16 mins

14 hrs 44 mins

The first answer above is more obvious: counting from lunchtime to bedtime.

The second answer comes from the possibility that we are counting from bedtime on one day to lunchtime on the next.

Notice how **the examples handle hours and minutes separately.**

- Because there are 60 minutes in an hour (not 100), you are likely to get into a tangle if you subtract the hours and minutes in one go.

Do not write 9.16 hours or 14.44 hours: **16 minutes are not 0.16 hours!**

14.

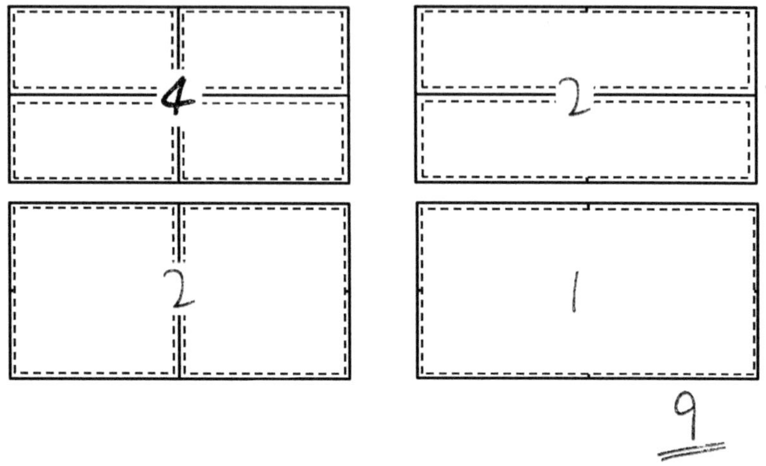

[Diagrams of rectangles divided with labels 4, 2, 2, 1, 2, 9]

15.

[Rectangle labelled 192 cm², 3x by x]

$3x \times x = 192$
$3x^2 = 192$
$x^2 = 64$
$x = 8$

[Rectangle with sides 3×8=24 and 8]

24
8
+ 24
8
64 cm

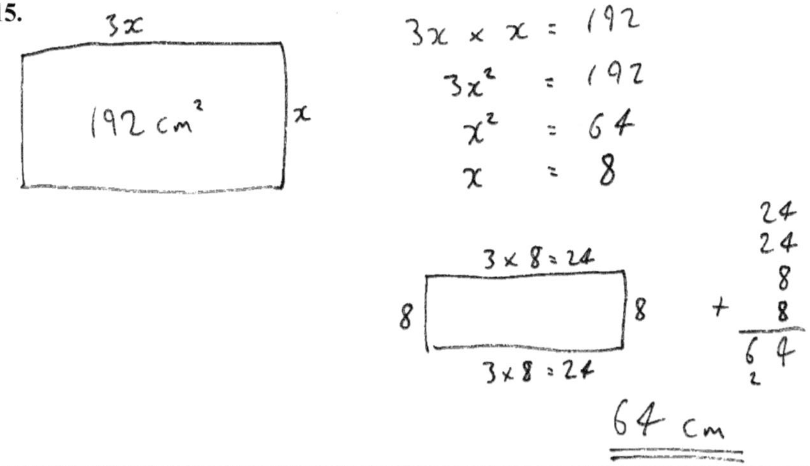

Algebra is far and away the best method for answering this question, which is why I haven't offered an alternative example, as I did for the algebra question in Paper 1.

However, you could also use **trial and improvement** (width 10cm is too large; width 5cm is too small; width 7cm is still too small; etc.).

16.

[Handwritten working showing four dots with labels:]
- ① a median of 3 ← middle number
- ② a mode of 2 ← must be 2 of them
- ③ a mean of 6   6 × 5 = 30 totals 30
- ④ a range of 12   2 + 12 = 14

Answer: 2, 2, 3, ..., 9, 14

- The **median is 3**, so this must go in the **middle space**.
- **2 is the mode**, so **there must be more than one** (the mode is the most common number – like *la mode* in French, which means 'fashion': it is the most 'fashionable' number in the set). There cannot be more than two of them, because there are only two spaces to the left of 3.
- The **range is the difference between the smallest and largest number**: if 2 is the smallest and the range is 12, **14 must be the largest**.
- You find the **mean by adding all the numbers together, then dividing by the number of numbers (5)**. If the mean is 6, the total of all the numbers must be **30**: so the missing number is **9**.

17. (a)

[Handwritten working:]
0.32 × 150

        150
      × 0.32

        300
       4500

      48.00 = 48

or

$\frac{16\cancel{32}}{\cancel{100}} \times \frac{\cancel{150}^{3}}{\cancel{2}_{1}} = \frac{48}{1} = 48$

Remember that 'of' means 'multiply'.

You could also find 1% of 150, then multiply this by 32.

(b)

100% − 15% = 85%.

0.85 × 85

        85
      × 0.85

        425
       6800

      72.25   £72.25

or

0.15 × 85

        85
      × 0.15

        425
        850

      12.75

    8⁷8.⁹0̸0̸
   − 12.75

     72.25   £72.25

As you can see, the first method involves less calculation and is more direct. For the **fraction method**, not shown above, see the discussion of **Paper 1, Q8**.

END

Paper 3: *Wazzoo!*

Challenging Level

Papers 3 and 4 include a number of wordy questions. They also require students to apply their knowledge to scenarios which may be unfamiliar. However, every question continues to test core Key Stage 2 skills.

---

1. What is 3034 – 2136?

Answer: ……………… **(2)**

---

2. What is 8483 × 8?

Answer: ……………… **(2)**

---

3. Complete the following calculations by filling in the boxes: **(6)**

(a)
```
   2 4 5 ▢
+  ▢ 8 2 1
---------
   9 2 ▢ 0
```

(b)
```
   5 0 ▢ 0
-    6 2 ▢
---------
   4 ▢ 3 5
```

4. **(a)** Find $\frac{3}{5}$ of 40.

Answer: .... **(2)**

(b) Find $\frac{6}{11}$ of 132.

Answer: .... **(2)**

5.
- I am less than 90
- I am a multiple of 18
- I am more than the product of 9 and 7

What number am I?

Answer: .... **(2)**

6. Which of these numbers is closest to 2.6?

   2.5   2.07   2.7   2.61   2.605   2.59

Answer: .... **(2)**

7. Write in figures the number thirty five thousand, five hundred and thirty.

Answer: ……………… **(1)**

8. Brianna has decided to swap the numbers on the door of her parents' hotel room:

4 1 4 2

Having unscrewed the metal digits, she must decide how to re-attach them.

Using all the digits:

(a) What is the smallest odd number that she could make?

Answer: ……………… **(1)**

(b) What is the largest number that she could make?

Answer: ……………… **(1)**

(c) How many <u>different</u> numbers could she make?

Answer: ……………… **(2)**

9. Levi, Lottie and Luciana share £60 in the same proportion as their ages.

   Levi has 3 times as much as Lottie, but half as much as Luciana.

   How much money does Levi have?

   Answer: .... (3)

10. Renting a speedboat costs £70 per hour plus a fixed charge of £40 for any length of rental.

   (a) Alessandro wants to rent a boat for 3 hours.

   How much should this cost him?

   Answer: .... (2)

   (b) Alessandro gets distracted and forgets to return the speedboat on time. When he eventually gives it back, he must pay £3610.

   How long did he have it for?

   Answer: .... (2)

11. Yesterday I baked a chocolate cake. I ate $\frac{1}{4}$ straight away, then gave half of the rest to my next door neighbour, Janice. I put the leftovers in the fridge.

(a) What fraction of the cake did I put in the fridge?

Answer: ……………… **(2)**

(b) If I gave 360g of cake to Janice, how much did I eat yesterday?

Answer: ……………… **(3)**

---

12. Complete the following sequences:

(a) 1   4   9   ___   ___   36

(b) 12   ___   2   -3   ___   -13

(c) -1   1   4   ___   13   ___

(6)

13. It takes 3 cats 4 weeks to catch 12 mice.

If all the cats catch mice at the same, steady rate:

(a) How long would it take the three cats to catch 18 mice?

Answer: ……………… **(2)**

(b) How many mice would 2 cats catch in 12 weeks?

Answer: ……………… **(3)**

---

14. Draw all the lines of symmetry on the following shapes:

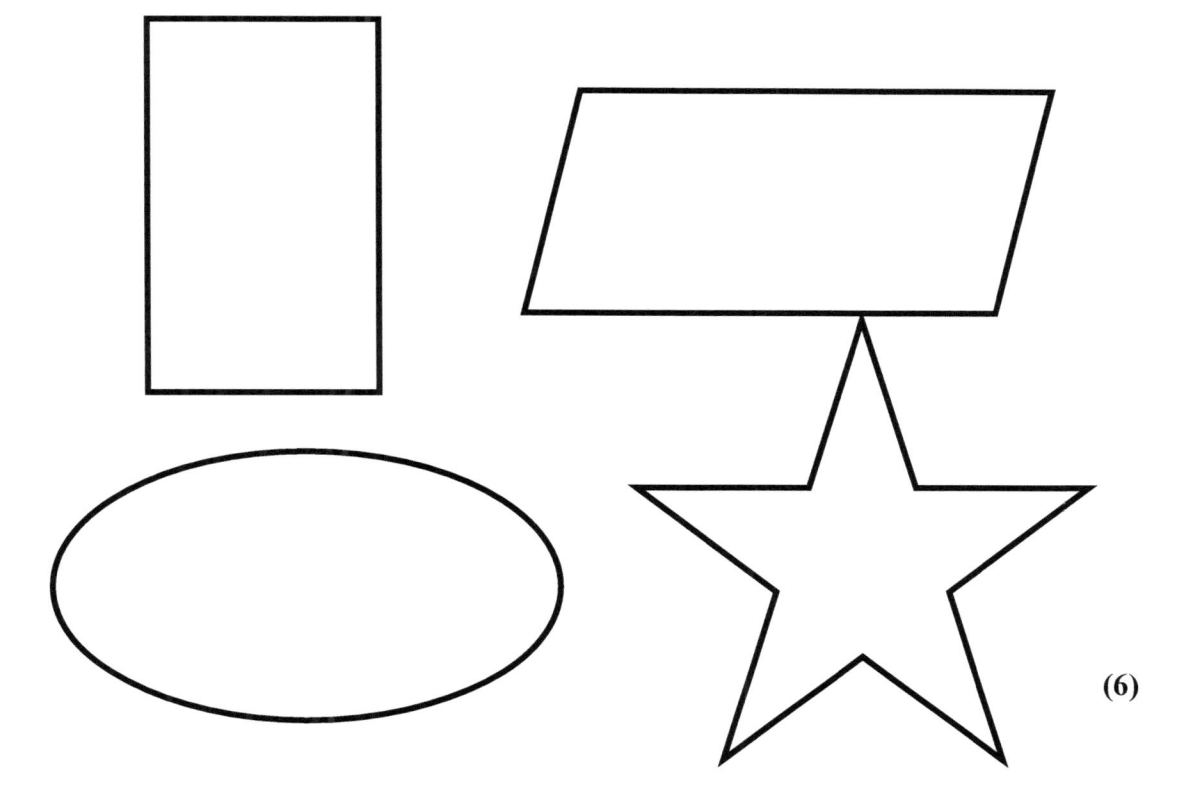

(6)

15. How many rectangles (not counting squares) can be found in each of these grids?

(a)

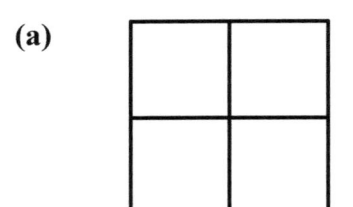

Answer: .... (2)

(b)

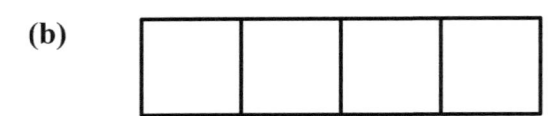

Answer: .... (2)

(c)

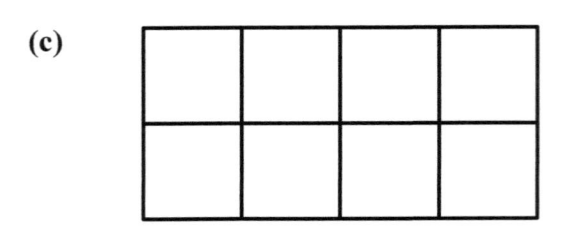

Answer: .... (4)

16. A *Wazzoo!* chocolate bar has these dimensions when packed tightly:

2 cm × 2 cm × 13 cm

I want to pack some in the following box:

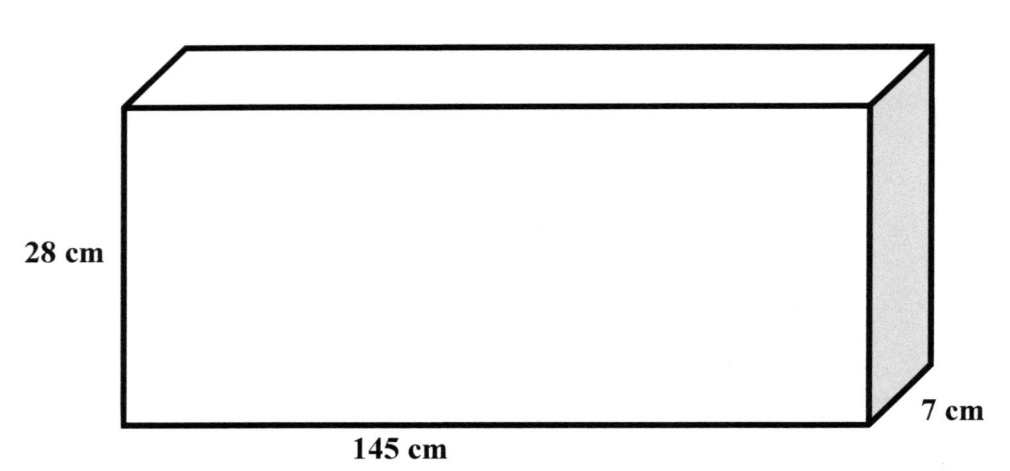

28 cm

145 cm

7 cm

What is the maximum number of *Wazzoo!* bars that I can pack:

(a) laying them on their sides?

Answer: ……………… **(3)**

(b) standing them on their ends?

Answer: ……………… **(3)**

(c) with some on their sides and some on their ends?

Answer: ……………… **(3)**

17. A and B are two corners of a triangle.

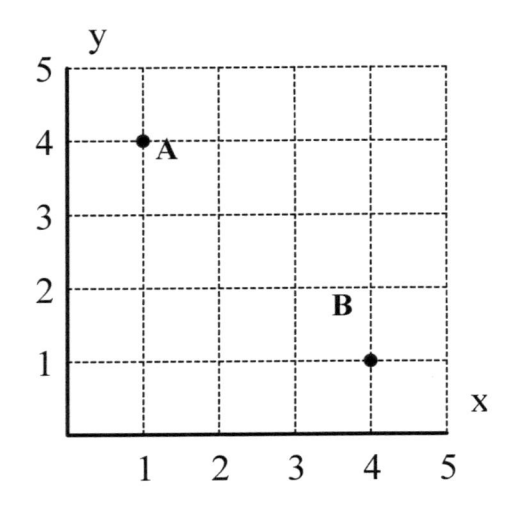

(a) Write down the coordinates of a third point, **C**, which would complete a right-angled isosceles triangle.

Answer: .... **(2)**

(b) Write down the coordinates of a different point **C**, which would complete a right angled triangle which is not isosceles.

Answer: .... **(2)**

(c) Write down the coordinates of a different point **C**, which would complete a scalene triangle.

Answer: .... **(2)**

---

18. Chadia has made a model of her school using wooden blocks:

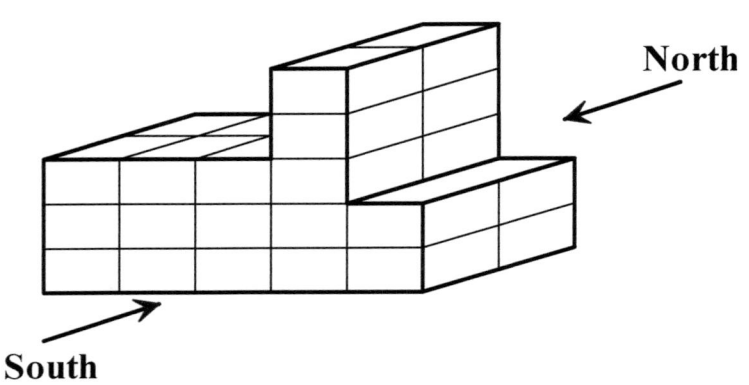

On the following grids, accurately draw the school as seen from:

The east

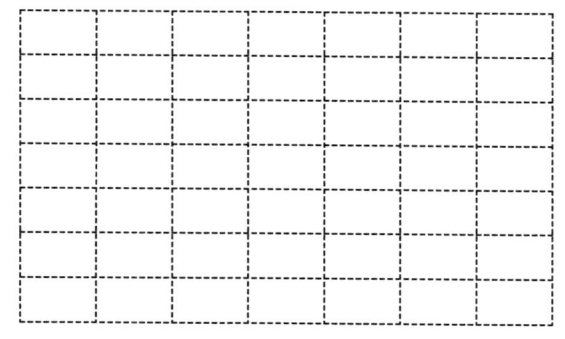

(2)

The north

(3)

---

19.   1 + 2 + 3 + 4 = 10

Make the calculations work by using only these symbols:

( )   +   −   ×   ÷

(a)   1   2   3   4   =   11

(b)   1   2   3   4   =   36

(c)   1   2   3   4   =   5   (6)

20. A die is a cube with the numbers 1 – 6 represented by dots, one number to each face. Each pair of opposite faces adds up to 7.

I lay 5 dice on the table in the following pattern:

I cannot see the numbers hidden between the dice, or between the dice and the table.

I walk round the table, adding together all the numbers that I can see.

(a) What is the largest total that I might count?

Answer: .... (3)

(b) What is the smallest total that I might count?

Answer: .... (3)

21. The instruction **q @ r** tells you to

- add 2 to **r**
- multiply the answer by **q**

For example, **5 @ 7**
means
$$5 \times (7 + 2)$$
$$= 5 \times 9$$
$$= 45$$

(a) Find **11 @ 9**

Answer: .... **(2)**

(b) **3 @ y = 12**

Find **y**

Answer: .... **(3)**

(c) **w @ w = 48**

Find **w**

Answer: .... **(3)**

TOTAL MARKS: 100

Paper 3: Wazzoo!

Solutions

1.
$$\overset{2\;\;9\;\;2\;\;1}{\cancel{3}\cancel{0}\cancel{3}\cancel{4}}$$
$$-2136$$
$$\overline{0898}$$

Notice how the 0 in the top line becomes 9, meaning that the 3 to its left must become 2.

$$\begin{array}{r}898\end{array}$$

2.
$$8483$$
$$\times\;\;\;\;8$$
$$\overline{67864}$$
$$\;\;\;_{3\;6\;2}$$

$$67864$$

3. (a)
$$\begin{array}{r}2\;4\;\boxed{5}\;\boxed{9}\\+\;\boxed{6}\;8\;2\;1\\\hline 9\;2\;\boxed{8}\;0\\_1\;\;\;\;\;_1\end{array}$$

(b) $$\begin{array}{r}\overset{4}{\cancel{5}}\;\overset{1}{0}\;\overset{1}{\cancel{6}}\;0\\-\;\;\;\;\;6\;2\;\boxed{5}\\\hline \boxed{4}\;4\;3\;5\end{array}$$

The best method here is to work carefully **from right to left**.

For example, looking at **(a)**:

- Something plus 1 equals 0; therefore, the 0 must be the second digit of 10, and the missing number at the top right must be 9. The 1 is then carried to the 'tens' column.
- $5 + 2 + 1 = 8$
- ... and so on.

4. (a)
or
$$\overset{3}{\cancel{9}}\times\frac{\overset{8}{\cancel{40}}}{\cancel{5}_1} = \frac{24}{1} = 24$$
$$8 \times 3 = 24$$

or
$$\frac{3}{5} = 0.6$$
$$\begin{array}{r}4\;0\\\times\;0.6\\\hline 2\;4\;0\\0\;0\\\hline 2\;4\;.0\end{array}$$

All the above methods are straightforward. It is helpful to have all three available to you.

(b)
$$\frac{6}{\cancel{11}_1}\times\frac{\overset{12}{\cancel{132}}}{1} = \frac{72}{1} = 72$$

Because 132 and 11 cancel (11 goes into 11 once, and into 132 12 times), this method works best here.

5.
$$9 \times 7 = 63$$
$$18\;\;36\;\;54\;\;\boxed{72}\;\;90$$
$$72$$
$$90$$

- Find 9×7 (which equals 63).
- Find a multiple of 18 which is greater than 63 and less than 90.

6.

$$2.500 \quad 2.070 \quad 2.700 \quad 2.610 \quad 2.605 \quad 2.590$$

Diffs: $0.100 \quad 0.530 \quad 0.100 \quad 0.010 \quad 0.005 \quad 0.010$

smallest

2.605

Because the longest number in the question has 3 decimal places, the method above involves **re-writing all the numbers to 3 d.p.** (by adding 0s).

Your next job is to **count the difference between each number and 2.6** (2.600), and choose **the number which gives the smallest difference.**

- You could save time by **crossing out all the obviously wrong answers** (such as 2.07, and perhaps 2.5 and 2.7), before using the above method.

7. 35 530

8. (a) 2 441

(b) 4 421

(c)
1 244   2 144   4 124   4 214   4 412
1 424   2 414   4 142   4 241   4 421
1 442   2 441

12

For part **(c)**, it is important to structure your working clearly, or you are likely to miss some combinations.

- Notice how the example begins with each digit in turn and **works systematically** through the possibilities.

9.

Method 1

Lottie	Levi	Luciana	Total
1	3	6	10 ↓×6
	(18)	6	60

£18

- For every £1 that Lottie has, Levi has £3 and Luciana has £6.
- This gives **a total of £10**.
- We know that they actually have £60 between them. To get from £10 to £60, we must **multiply by 6**.
- Therefore each number in the first row must be multiplied by 6 to get the real amount of money that each person has.
- $£3 × 6 = £18$

Method 2

Let Levi's amount = x

$x + \dfrac{x}{3} + 2x = 60$

Levi — Lottie — Luciana

$3x + \dfrac{x}{3} = 60 \quad \dfrac{9x}{3} + \dfrac{x}{3} = 60 \quad \dfrac{10x}{3} = 60$

$10x = 180$

$x = \dfrac{180}{10} = 18 \quad £18$

For this question, **Method 1** is probably more convenient.

10. (a)

$3 \times 70 + 40 = 210 + 40 = \underline{£250}$

- You need to multiply the number of hours by 70 and then add 40.
- **Don't forget the units (£) or you will lose a mark!**

(b)

$70t + 40 = 3610$

$70t = 3570$

$t = \dfrac{3570}{70} = \dfrac{357}{7}$

$7\overline{)357} = 51$

$\underline{51 \text{ hrs}}$

£70 × the number of hours ←──── £40 fixed charge

- t represents the amount of time for which the speedboat is hired, in hours.
- You could solve this **without using algebra**, by subtracting 40 and then dividing by 70. However, this would essentially be the same method: I have not given it as a separate example.

For a similar algebraic method, see **Paper 1, Q10 (a)**.

11. (a)

$1 - \dfrac{1}{4} = \dfrac{3}{4} \qquad \dfrac{3}{4} \div 2 = \dfrac{3}{4} \times \dfrac{1}{2} = \underline{\dfrac{3}{8}}$

Always check that your final answer cannot be simplified (reduced).

(b)

(Pie chart: three equal sections of 360g each; calculation $360 \times 2 = 720$; $3\overline{)720} = 240$; answer $\underline{240g}$)

- I gave the same amount to Janice as I put in the fridge: if I gave her 360g of cake, I put 360g in the fridge.
- $2 \times 360 = 720g$
- 720g is $\dfrac{3}{4}$ of the cake.
- Therefore $\dfrac{1}{4}$ of the cake is $720 \div 3$, which equals 240g.

If you are dealing with parts of an object, such as a cake, it can be very helpful to sketch the object: it will allow you to remain clear about what you are doing.

12.

(a) $1^{12}\qquad 4\,2^t\qquad 9\,3^t\qquad 16\qquad 25\qquad 36$

(b) $12\quad -5\quad 7\quad -5\quad 2\quad -5\quad -3\quad -5\quad -8\quad -5\quad -13$

(c) $-1\quad +2\quad 1\quad +3\quad 4\quad +4\quad 8\quad +5\quad 13\quad +6\quad 19$

(a) You need to become familiar with sequences of square and cube numbers, so that you can spot them before you waste a lot of time writing in differences.

(b) You may need to try a few possible differences before you find one that works.

(c) This is likely to be slightly more straightforward.

13. **Method 1**

Cats	Weeks	Mice
3	4 →×1.5 ⑥	12 →×1.5 18
3	12	×2 ⟨ 9→ 6
×2/3 ⟨ 3	12	×2/3 ㉔
2		

(a) 18 mice is 1.5 × 12 mice.
- Therefore the cats will take <u>1.5 × 4 weeks</u> to catch the mice.

6 weeks

(b) Only change **one thing at a time**.
- In 12 weeks, **3 cats** would catch 36 mice (18 × 2).
- In the same length of time, **2 cats** would catch $\frac{2}{3}$ as many mice as 3 cats.
- $\frac{2}{3}$ of 36 is 24.

24 mice

Method 2

Find out how many mice **1 cat** would catch in **1 week**:

Cats	Weeks	Mice
3 (÷3)	4	12 (÷3)
1	4 (÷4)	4 (÷4)
1	1	1

(a) How many weeks for **1 cat** to catch **18 mice**?
... and for **3 cats**?

| 1 (×3) | 18 (÷3) | 18 |
| 3 | ⑥ | 18 |

(b) How many mice would **2 cats** catch in **a week**?
... and in 12 weeks?

1 (×2)	1	1 (×2)
2	1 (×12)	2 (×12) ㉔
2	12	

14.

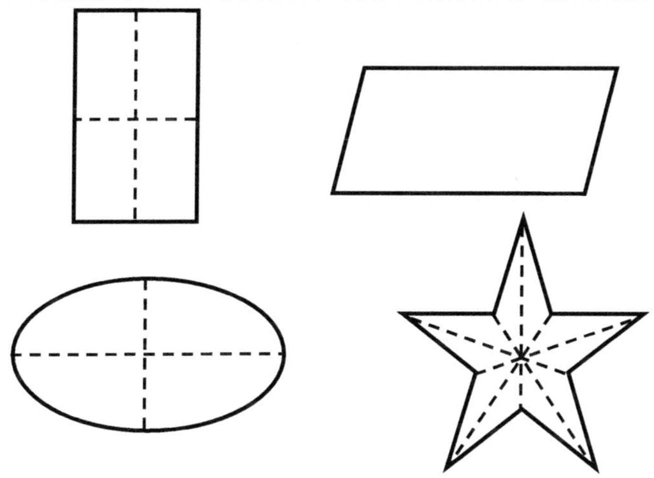

Deduct 1 mark for each missing line, or for each extra, incorrect line.

15. (a)

[Diagrams showing rectangles with numbers: 2, 2, 4; 3, 2, 6; and answer = 4]

(b)

[Diagrams showing: 1, 2, 4; 6, 2, 4; = 6]

(c)

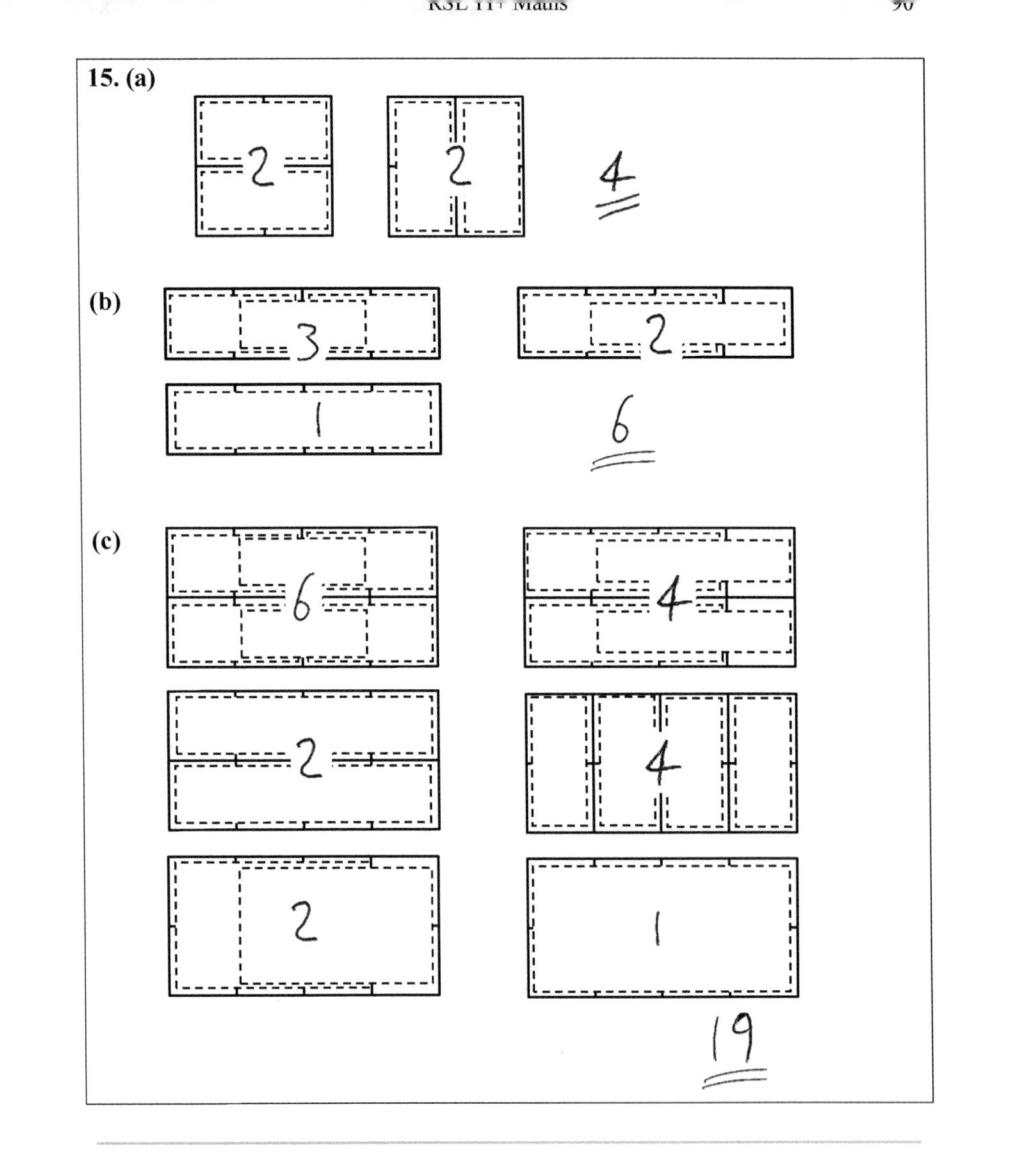

[Diagrams showing: 2, 1; = 19]

16. (a)

[Diagram of base showing 14.5 cm × 7 cm, with working:
- 14.5 / 2 = ... 3 remainder 1, giving 2 bars across, etc.
- 3 × 11 = 33 in the bottom layer
- Height: 28 cm / 2 = 14 layers
- 33 × 14 = 462 bars]

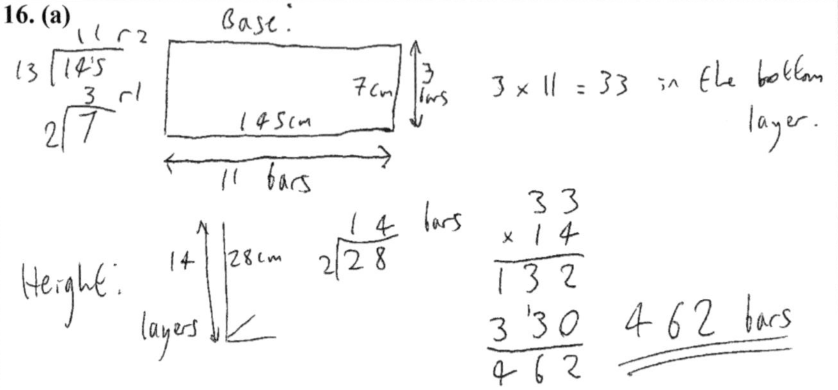

- You need to find how many bars can be laid in the base (33) of the box, then multiply this by the number that can be stacked on top of each other (14).

  (Alternatively, you could find out how many fit against the front face and multiply this by the number of times this can be repeated from front to back [3]; or find out how many fit in the end, and multiply this by the number that fit along the length [11]).

- Finding the volume of the box then dividing this by the volume of a bar **is NOT a correct method**: differently shaped objects with the same volume are not equivalent.

- For example, a bar of 0.5 cm × 0.5 cm × 208 cm would have the same volume as a *Wazzoo!* bar, but no such long bar would fit in the box.

(b)

[Diagram: Rectangle labelled "Base" with dimensions 7cm, 145cm, showing "3 bars" and "72 bars"]

$72 \times 3 = 216$ in bottom layer

Height: $2 \overline{)28}$ cm   2 layers

$\begin{array}{r} 216 \\ \times 2 \\ \hline 432 \end{array}$

432 bars

The same method applies here.

(c) CORRECT:

[Diagram: box with 28cm height, 7cm, showing "2 bars", "3 bars", "3 × 2 = 6"]

$462 + 6 = 468$ bars

INCORRECT:

$\begin{array}{r} 432 \\ + 33 \\ \hline 465 \end{array}$

465 bars

CORRECT:

- The solution to **(a)** leaves a 2cm gap at the end of the box.
- In this gap, it is possible to fit 6 bars standing on their ends.
- Therefore the maximum number of bars can be found **by adding 6 to the solution to (a)**.

INCORRECT:

- The solution to **(b)** leaves a 2 cm high gap above the bars.
- A single layer of 33 bars on their sides, as shown in the working for **(a)**, is 2 cm high.
- Therefore the maximum number of bars can be fitted in by adding 33 to the solution to **(b)**.

The incorrect answer above would still receive 2 marks.

A solution to **(c)** which uses incorrect numbers from **(a)** and/or **(b)**, but which is otherwise correct in itself, should receive all three marks. (Follow-through marking.)

17. (a) $(1, 1)$ **or** $(4, 4)$

An isosceles triangle has two sides of equal length. The right-angle must be at the point where the two equal lines meet, because there can be a maximum of one right-angle in a triangle.

If the triangle is right-angled or isosceles, but not both, it should be worth a mark.

(b) $(0, 3)$ **or** $(2, 5)$ **or** $(3, 0)$ **or** $(5, 2)$

If your triangle **is** isosceles, it should receive one mark.

(c) Any coordinate on the grid could be correct, **apart from** (0, 0), (1, 1) (2, 2), (3, 3), (4, 4) and (5, 5). Remember that your point **C** needs to be different from your answer to **(b)**.

18.   The east

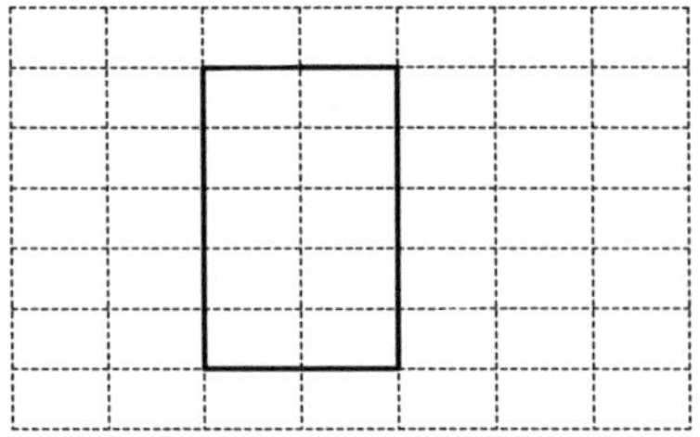

The north

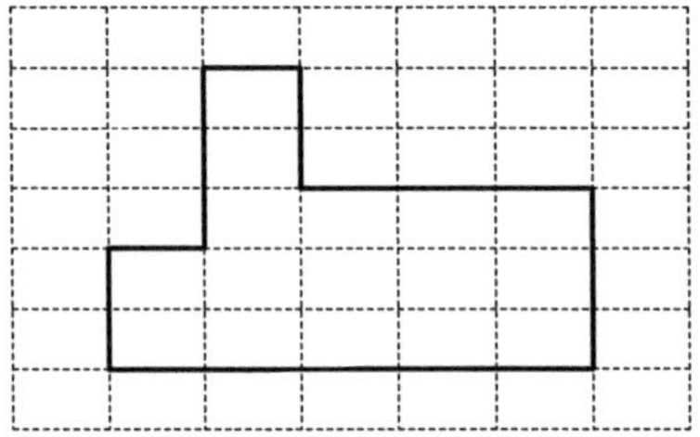

If your drawing from the east is twice as wide (4 units rather than 2), because the blocks in the 3D image look longer from front to back, this should also be acceptable.

19.   (a)   1 + 2 × 3 + 4 = 11
      (b)   (1 + 2) × 3 × 4 = 36
      (c)   (1 + 2) × 3 − 4 = 5

(a) could also be 1 − 2 + 3 × 4

20. (a)
Hide: 1, 2, 3, 4, 5   (middle die)   Total: 15
      1, 2   (each other die) × 4 Total: 12
7 × 3 = 21 dots on a die   2 × 5 = 10s   15
                                              27
                            7 × 8
                            = 27
                            78

There are 21 dots on a die, so there are 21 × 5 = 105 dots on 5 dice. This method involves hiding all the lowest value faces (especially 1 and 2), adding up the remaining faces, and subtracting them from 105.

- The middle die should just show 6, pointing upwards: **1, 2, 3, 4 and 5 are hidden**, making a total of 15.
- Each of the other 4 dice has **two hidden faces**: these should be **1 and 2**. This gives a total of 12.
- 15 + 12 = 27
- **Take 27 from the total number of dots on 5 dice (105), to give 78.**

You could also solve this question by adding up the faces which you **could** see.

(b)
Hide: 2, 3, 4, 5, 6   (middle die)   Total: 20
      6, 5   (each other die) × 4 Total: 44
                                          64
                                          105
                                          − 64
                                           41

This is the same method, but hiding the high values rather than the low ones.

21. (a)

$$11 \times (4+2) = 11 \times 11 = 121$$

This question is testing your ability to understand and apply a new mathematical rule. Before answering a question like this, **read the question's example repeatedly until you fully understand the rule.**

(b) Method 1: algebra

$$3 \times (y + 2) = 12$$
$$y + 2 = \frac{12}{3} = 4$$
$$y = 4 - 2 = \underline{\underline{2}}$$

Method 2: trial and improvement

$$3 \times (\square + 2) = 12$$
$$5 \quad " \quad " = 21 \quad \times$$
$$3 \quad " \quad " = 15 \quad \times$$
$$2 \quad " \quad " = 12 \quad \checkmark \quad y = \underline{\underline{2}}$$

The advantage of **Method 1** is that it will produce an exact answer even if it is not a whole number. This would take a long time with **Method 2**.

(c)

$$\square \times (\square + 2) = 48$$
$$5 \quad " \quad " = 35 \quad \times$$
$$7 \quad " \quad " = 63 \quad \times$$
$$6 \quad " \quad " = 48 \quad \checkmark \quad n = \underline{\underline{6}}$$

You probably will not have learnt the method for solving this problem using algebra (you can expect to study it in year 8 or 9). Therefore trial and improvement is the best method.

It is best to **shoot low then high** (or vice versa) **and then zoom in** until you find the answer. Set your working out clearly in columns, so that you don't lose track. Don't guess randomly and scatter your working across the page!

With a fiddly question of this sort, it is very likely that the answer will be a whole number. Despite all the contrary evidence, examiners are rarely evil.

END

Paper 4: *Roderick the Cart Horse*
Challenging Level

1. What is 487 + 709?

   Answer: .... **(2)**

2. What is 6664 ÷ 4?

   Answer: .... **(2)**

3. What is 4.2 ÷ 0.7?

   Answer: .... **(2)**

4. I pour three 1.22 litre jugs of orange juice into a bucket which has a capacity of 5 litres. How much of the bucket is not filled? Give your answer in ml.

   Answer: .... **(2)**

5. (a) Write down 2 ways of making exactly £1.10 using 5 coins.

   Answer 1: .... **(1)**

   Answer 2: .... **(1)**

(b) Is it possible to make £1.20 with 4 or more coins, without using any kind of coin twice? Show your working.

Answer: .... **(2)**

6. Complete the empty boxes in the following table:

Percentage	Fraction (simplest form)	Decimal
20 %		0.2
		1.5
7 %		
	$\frac{3}{8}$	

(7)

7.

(a)
```
   □ □ 6
 ×     5
 -------
 1 2 3 □
```

(b)
```
      0 7 □ 6
    _____
  8 ) □ 6 4 □
```

(6)

8. Calculate the new price of each of the following products:

   (a) 12.5 % off all prices!   £48

   Answer: .... (3)

   (b) Owing to high demand, all prices are 20% higher than on the tag.   £15

   Answer: .... (3)

9. Joy the cow steals 60 % of Roderick the cart horse's dinner. When Roderick comes back to his trough, only 5 kg of food is left.

   How much food did Roderick have originally?

   Answer: .... (3)

10. Rewrite the following numbers in order from smallest to largest:

0.4 $\frac{4}{11}$ $\frac{1}{3}$ 0.3 $\frac{5}{4}$

………   ………   ………   ………   ………   **(3)**

---

11. Which of these numbers is closest to 0.85?

0.86   0.846   0.8522   0.84   0.8479

Answer: ……………… **(2)**

---

12. Jo is buying animals for her new petting zoo. She makes the following calculations:

- 3 rabbits, 1 rat and 1 raccoon would cost £44.15
- 1 rabbit, 2 rats and 3 raccoons would cost £62.30
- 1 rabbit, 2 rats and 1 raccoon would cost £30.30

How much would 1 rabbit, 1 rat and 1 raccoon cost altogether?

Answer: ……………… **(3)**

13. When Kwasi boards the sleeper train at Berlin, his watch shows the following time:

20:18

He wakes up as the train pulls in at Milan Central the next morning. The station clock shows

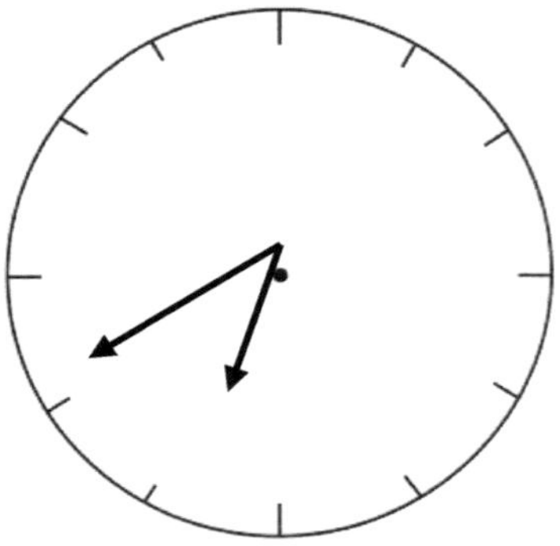

How long was Kwasi's journey?

Answer: ……………… **(3)**

---

14. Nirvana Cocktail Emporium has invented a new drink: the Monstermont Martini. It contains:

- 3 parts gin
- 1 part vermouth
- 1 part liquidized Brussels sprouts
- 2 parts vodka

(a) If a drink contains 60 ml of vodka:-

(i) how much gin does it contain?

Answer: ……………… **(2)**

(ii) what is the volume of the entire drink?

Answer: ……………… **(2)**

(b) Jean-Claude sips his cocktail at a steady rate of 45 ml per minute.

How long will it take him to finish the drink?

Answer: ……………… **(3)**

15. Mrs Tiggywinkle is trying to arrange her class into groups.

- She puts them into groups of 3, but there are 2 left over.
- She puts them into groups of 5, but there are 3 left over.
- She puts them into groups of 6, but there are 5 left over.

There are fewer than 40 children in the class. How many are there?

Answer: ……………… **(3)**

16. Solve the following equations:

(a) $3x - 12 = 3$

Answer: $x =$ .... (2)

(b) $y^2 - 16 = 0$

Answer: $y =$ .... (2)

17. If the total area of the following shape is 300 cm², what is its perimeter?

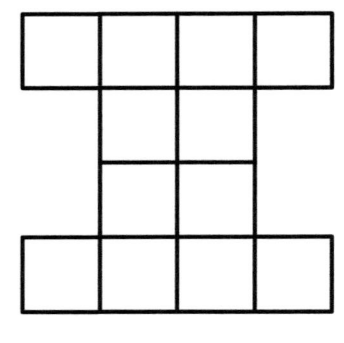

(Not actual size)

Answer: .... (4)

18. Re-arrange the digits 2, 3, 0 and 4 to make the largest possible four-digit number which divides exactly by 7.

Answer: **4032** (2)

19. Triangle ABC has these measurements:
- AB is 5 cm long
- Angle A is 40°
- AC is 4 cm long

A ├─────────────────────────────

(a) Complete triangle ABC. (3)

(b) What is the size of angle C?   Answer: **87°** (approximately) (2)

20. Each number in the triangles below is the product of the two numbers directly beneath it.

For example:

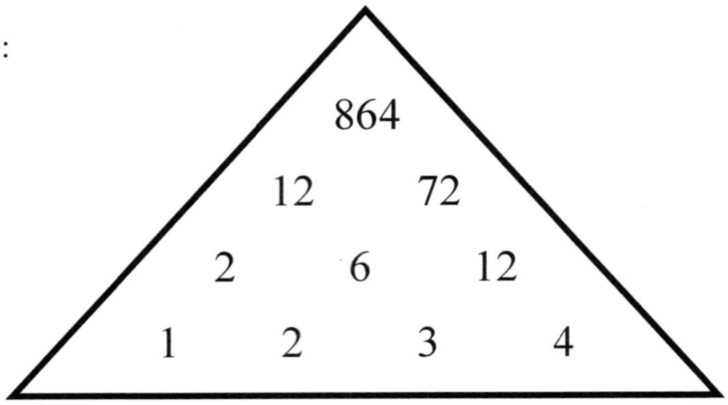

```
            864
         12     72
        2    6    12
       1   2    3    4
```

Complete the following triangles using whole numbers:

(a)

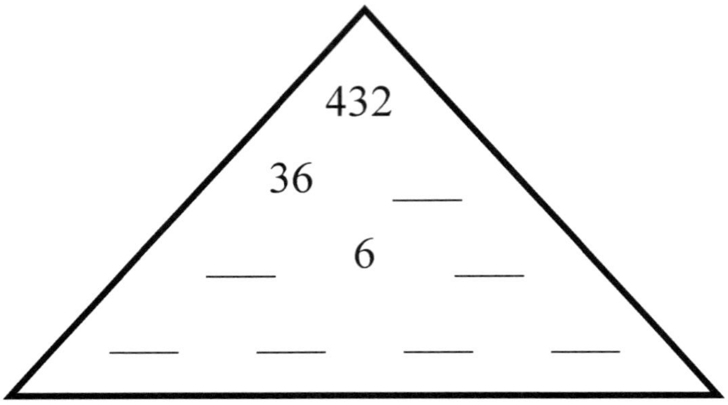

```
           432
         36    ___
       ___   6    ___
     ___  ___  ___  ___
```

(2)

(b)

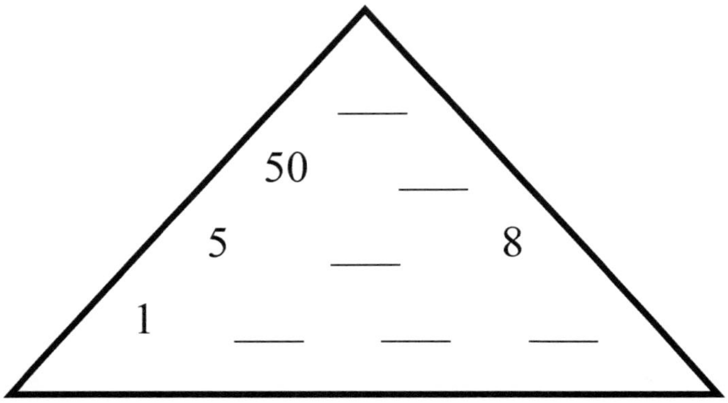

```
          ___
        50    ___
      5    ___    8
     1  ___  ___  ___
```

(2)

21. Nicola and Alec would like to build a 154 km wall. They calculate that it would take 1000 builders 6 months to complete the job.

(a) If every person builds the same amount of wall each month, how many builders would be needed to finish the wall in 4 months?

Answer: ……………… **(2)**

(b) Nicola and Alec do not want to pay 1000 builders, so they decide to build the wall by themselves. Alec works at $\frac{1}{3}$ of the speed of a builder. Nicola works twice as fast as Alec.

How long would it take the two of them to complete the wall?

Answer: ……………… **(4)**

22. Stephanie has decided to get fit before a walking holiday, so she goes for a jog. She runs straight down the road as far as the petrol station, then turns round and runs straight back home.

Here is a graph which shows her distance from home during the run:

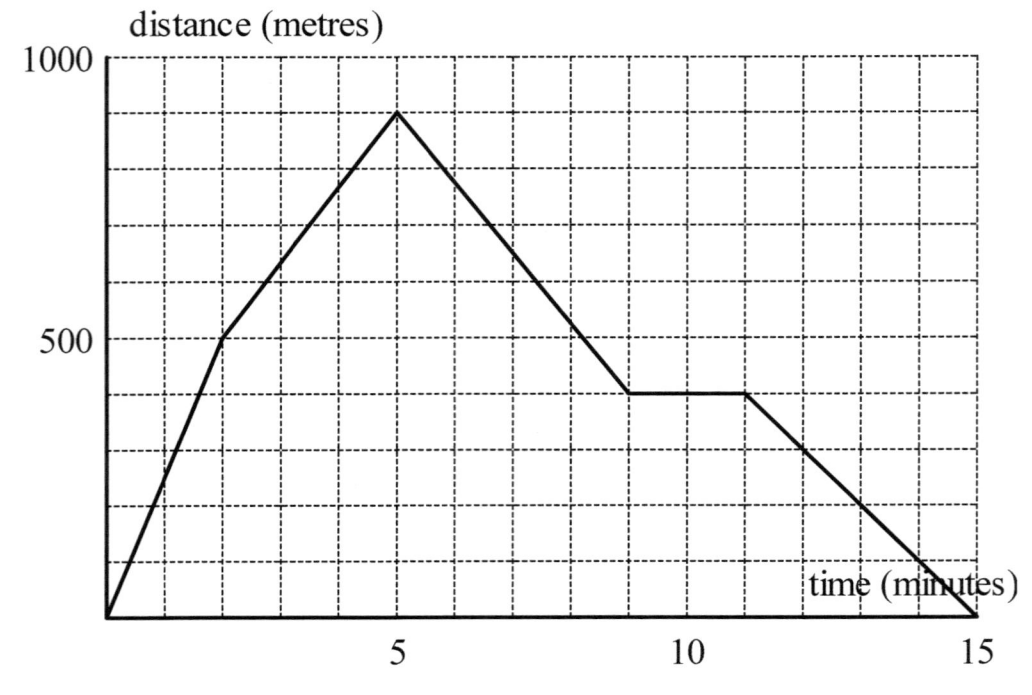

(a) How far from Stephanie's home is the petrol station?

Answer: ……………………… **(1)**

(b) During which time period does Stephanie run fastest?

Answer: ……………………… **(2)**

(c) Describe what happens in the first five minutes.

Answer: ……………………………………………………………………………………
……………………………………………………………………...……………………… **(2)**

(d) **(i)** What is Stephanie's average speed in metres per minute on her way to the petrol station?

Answer: ……………………… **(2)**

(ii) What is Stephanie's average speed on the way back from the petrol station, **leaving out** the time when she stops at Burger King to eat some chips?

Answer: .... **(3)**

---

23. Complete the following sequences:

(a) 100   93   87   82   ____   ____

(b) 5   7   11   19   ____   ____

(c) 216   125   ____   27   ____   1

(6)

---

24. Work out which digit from 1 – 9 is represented by each symbol in the equations below.

☼ – ♪ = ➔   ✉ × ✉ = ✉ + ✉

✉ + ☎ = ♪   ◀ – ☺ = ✉ – ♣

☎ × ☎ = Δ + ♣ = ☼   ♣ × ♣ = ♣

☼ = ____   ♪ = ____   ➔ = ____   ✉ = ____   ☎ = ____

Δ = ____   ♣ = ____   ◀ = ____   ☺ = ____

(4)

TOTAL MARKS: 100

Paper 4: Roderick the Cart Horse

Solutions

1.
$$\begin{array}{r} 487 \\ +709 \\ \hline 1196 \end{array} \quad \underline{1196}$$

2.
$$4\overline{)6^2 6^2 6 4} \quad \underline{1666}$$

3.
$$\frac{4.2}{0.7}{\scriptsize(\times 10) \atop (\times 10)} = \frac{42}{7} = \underline{6}$$

- Multiply the top and bottom of the fraction by 10, 100, 1000 … whatever is necessary to remove the decimal points. (Be careful always to **multiply top and bottom by the same amount**.)
- Cancel / reduce as far as you can.
- When you can cancel no further, **it may then be necessary to perform a division calculation** in the usual way.

When a division contains **at least one decimal**, it is helpful to begin **by writing it in the form of a fraction**.

4.
$$\begin{array}{r} {\scriptstyle 7\ 9} \\ \cancel{8}.\cancel{\emptyset}\cancel{\emptyset} \\ -3.66 \\ \hline 1.34 \end{array} \qquad \begin{array}{r} 1.22 \\ \times\ 3 \\ \hline 3.66 \end{array} \qquad 1.34L = \underline{1340\,ml}$$

5. (a)
50p, 20p, 20p, 10p, 10p
£1, 5p, 2p, 2p, 1p

Notice that the question doesn't require you to use different coins.

(b)
£1, 10p, 5p, 2p, 2p, 1p   NO
50p, 20p, 10p, 5p...   NO
£1, 20p   NO   not possible

This working demonstrates fully that it is not possible, by starting first with £1 and showing that you must repeat a coin; then with 50p and showing that you cannot get as far as £1.20 while using different coins; then with £1 again, showing that it is possible to reach £1.20, but with fewer than 4 coins.

However, any reasonable working is likely to be acceptable, even if it is not complete.

6.

Percentage	Fraction (simplest form)	Decimal
20 %	$\frac{20}{100} = \frac{1}{5}$	0.2
150%	$\frac{1.5}{1} = \frac{3}{2}$ Or $1\frac{1}{2}$	1.5
7 %	$\frac{7}{100}$	0.07
37.5 %	$\frac{3}{8}$	0.375

$8\overline{)3.0^30^60^40}$ → 0.375

7.

(a)
```
    [2] 4 [6]
  ×       5
  ─────────
  1 2 3 [0]
```

(b)
```
        0 7 [0] 6
      ┌─────────
    8 │ 5 6 4 8
```

There are often several logical routes through these questions.

For example, looking at (a), you might begin by calculating 5 × 6, then working through from the right. Alternatively:

- Once you know that the bottom right box is 0, you could work out 1230 ÷ 5.
- As the answer is more than 1000 but less than 1500, the top left number must be 2 (because 5 × 200 = 1000, but 5 × 300 = 1500).

The starting point for (b) is to recognise that the two-digit number ending in 6, which 8 goes into 7 times, is 56.

---

8. (a)

$100\% - 12.5\% = 87.5\%$

```
    0.875
  ×    48
  ───────
   7.000
  35.000
  ───────
  42.000
```

£42

For a discussion of this and other methods, see **Paper 1, Q8 (b)** and **Paper 2, Q17 (b)**.

(b) $100\% + 20\% = 120\%$

```
    15
  × 1.2
  ─────
    30
   150
  ─────
   18.0
```

£18

Perhaps the most difficult thing here is to keep the courage of your convictions and use exactly the same method as in (a)!

- The principle behind percentage increase is **the same** as for percentage decrease.

9.

$100\% - 60\% = 40\% = 0.4$

Before $\underset{\div 0.4}{\overset{\times 0.4}{\rightleftarrows}}$ 5kg

$\dfrac{5}{0.4} = \dfrac{50}{4} = \dfrac{25}{2} = \underline{\underline{12.5 \text{ kg}}}$

If you got this right, congratulations: this is a kind of problem which many students find difficult.

The method above can be summarized as follows:

- We need to **reverse a percentage change**.
- What **decimal** was the original amount **multiplied by** to produce the new amount? (Answer: 0.4)
- Reverse this by **dividing** the new amount by 0.4.

See **Q3** above for some thoughts on dividing by decimals.

DO NOT find 60 % of 5 kg and add this to 5 kg! 60 % of 5 kg will not be the same as 60 % of the original amount, so this approach will **always** produce a wrong answer.

There are other ways of solving this problem, but they are much fiddlier. I strongly recommend that you become familiar with the method shown above.

10.

0.4 $\dfrac{4}{11}$ 0.33... $\dfrac{1}{3}$ 0.30 $\dfrac{5}{4}$ 1.25

0.40   0.36... 0.3 4)5.00

$11\overline{)4.00}$

0.3, $\dfrac{1}{3}$, $\dfrac{4}{11}$, 0.4, $\dfrac{5}{4}$

This method involves converting each number into a decimal (here, all to 2 decimal places), so as to make the comparison simple.

- Notice the method of **converting a fraction to a decimal: dividing the top** (the numerator) **by the bottom** (the denominator).

11.

0.86   0.846   0.8522   0.84   0.8479

It is sensible to begin by **eliminating the obviously incorrect options**.

- 0.86 and 0.84 are clearly further away than the others.
- 0.846 is obviously further away than 0.8479.

Next you need to find the difference between each of the remaining options and 0.85. The smaller difference wins!

$0.8522 \qquad 0.8500$
$-0.8500 \qquad -0.8479$
$\overline{0.0022} \qquad \overline{0.0021}$

$\underline{\underline{0.8479}}$

Remember to write your final answers in the form given in the question, i.e. as fractions, decimals or percentages, as appropriate.

For a slightly different approach, see **Paper 1, Q9**.

12.

3 rab + 1 cow + 1 cat = 44.15
1 rab + 2 rab + 3 rab = 62.30
1 rab + 2 rab + 1 cow = 30.30

5 rab + 5 rab + 5 rab = (36.75
$\div 5 \qquad \div 5 \qquad \div 5$
1 rab + 1 cow + 1 cat = $\underline{\underline{£27.35}}$

27.35
$5)\overline{(136.75}$

This question is designed to look more complicated than it really is!

- **You do not need to find the individual prices of the animals.**

If you **add everything together** you will have the cost of buying **5 of each type** of animal: **divide the total price by 5**, and you have the cost of buying 1 of each.

Sometimes a question will seem to require algebra, when in fact there is a more convenient approach available.

13.

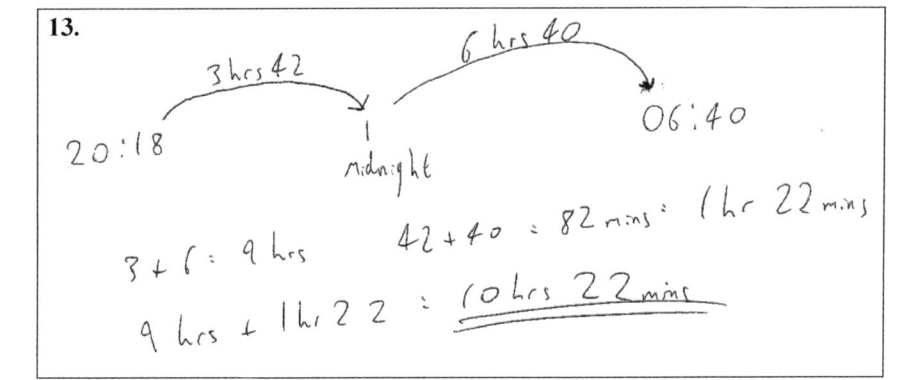

20:18 → 3 hrs 42 → midnight → 6 hrs 40 → 06:40

3 + 6 = 9 hrs   42 + 40 = 82 mins = 1 hr 22 mins

9 hrs + 1 hr 22 = 10 hrs 22 mins

Number lines are very useful when dealing with time.

Resist the temptation to add or subtract times using the column method (as used for example in **Question 1**). This is because seconds and minutes work in groups of 60, not 100.

---

14. (a)

Gin	Vermouth	Sprouts	Vodka	Total
3	1	1	2 (×30)	7
90ml	30ml	30ml	60ml	210ml

(i) 90 ml

(ii) 210 ml

The Monsermont Martini sounds revolting. The main lesson of this question is to avoid drinks with weird names.

A less important lesson is to **arrange proportion/ratio questions in a table**. This keeps things simple and logical. **Include a 'Total' column.**

- Set out **the original proportions**, as given in the question.
- In a new row, **add the next piece of information** (60 ml of vodka).
- Work out **what multiple gets you from the first row to the second** and write this down (2 × **30** = 60).
- **Apply this multiple to the other columns** (multiply everything by 30).

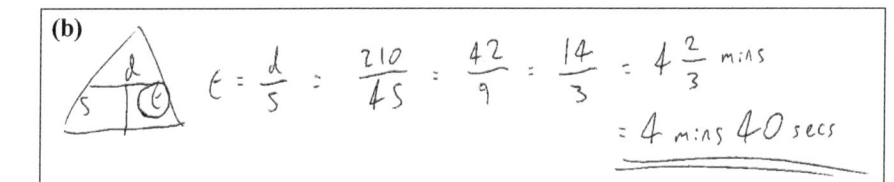

(b)

$t = \dfrac{d}{s} = \dfrac{210}{45} = \dfrac{42}{9} = \dfrac{14}{3} = 4\dfrac{2}{3}$ mins

$= 4$ mins 40 secs

The example uses the '**Speed Distance Time Triangle**' explained in **Paper 1, Q13 (b) (iii)**, to work out that **time** $= \dfrac{distance}{speed}$.

- In this case, '**distance**' means '**amount drunk**'.

If you get a decimal answer (4.67, to 2 decimal places), **be careful: decimals are not the same as seconds**. You should find the time by working out 0.67 × 60 which gives 40 (to the nearest second).

15.

The '6 + 5 times table': 11, 17, 23, 29, 35
'5 + 3': 8, 13, 18, 23
'3 + 2': 23 ← (7×3 + 2)

23

Because there are 5 people left over when Mrs Tiggywinkle puts her class into groups of 6, the number of children must be **5 more than a number in the 6 times table** – and so on.

The example starts with the '6 + 5 times table', because this gives fewest options. By the time you have found a number in both the '6 + 5' and '5 + 3' lists, you only need to check whether this also fits in the '3 + 2' row.

You could start with the '3 + 2 times table', but this would take longer because there are more possibilities.

16. (a)

$3x - 12 = 3$
$3x = 15$ (+12)
$x = 5$ (÷3)

(b)

$y^2 - 16 = 0$
$y^2 = 16$ (+16)
$y = \sqrt{16} = 4$

−4 is also a correct answer to **(b)**, because $(-4)^2$ also equals 16.

It is fairly unusual for an 11+ paper to set an equation with a squared variable (y^2), such as in **(b)**. However, these are not difficult to handle once you understand how to solve a simple equation.

17.

$\frac{300}{12} = \frac{100}{4} = 25 \text{ cm}^2$ (area of 1 square)

$\sqrt{25} = 5 \text{ cm}$ (1 side of 1 square) [25 cm² ↕ 5 cm]

$5 \times 20 = 100 \text{ cm}$

If you would like more help with algebra, it is worth flicking back through this pack, where several similar solutions are explained in more depth. For example, see **Paper 1, Q10**.

This is simple if you have a clear system, working a step at a time.

- If the area of one square is 25 cm², **one side of one square is 5 cm** long.
- The perimeter is **20 units long**, so the total perimeter is 100 cm.

18.

7 | 4320 r1   6 | 720 r1
   617 r1   7 | 4320 r2   ×   7 | 230 r2 × 7 | 4032 ✓
             7 | 4203   576   604 r2
             600 r3   57 r2   4032
                           4032 ✓

This is the sort of question that can waste a lot of time for few marks. In a timed exam, I would **skip it and return to it at the end**.

Make sure that you work down from the largest number, without missing one out (it might be the one you are looking for).

19. (a)

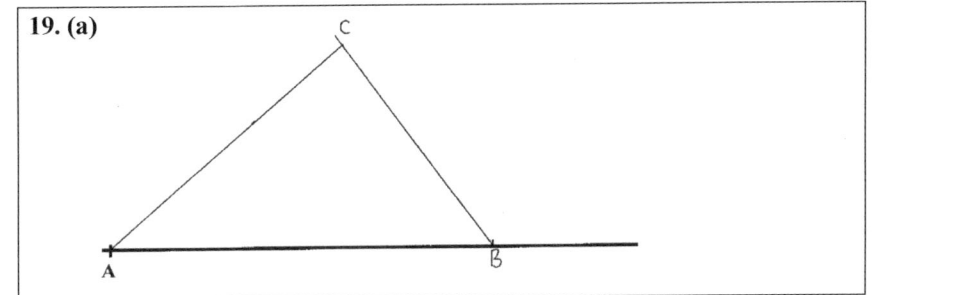

[Diagram of triangle with vertices A, B, C]

You will lose marks if your lines are inaccurate by more than 1 or 2 mm, and likewise if the angles are more than a degree or two out.

(b) 87°

Any answer which is more than 85° and less than 90° is likely to be acceptable, but to be safe you should be between 86° and 88°.

Lengths in the example answer may be slightly inaccurate, owing to printing adjustments.

---

20. (a)

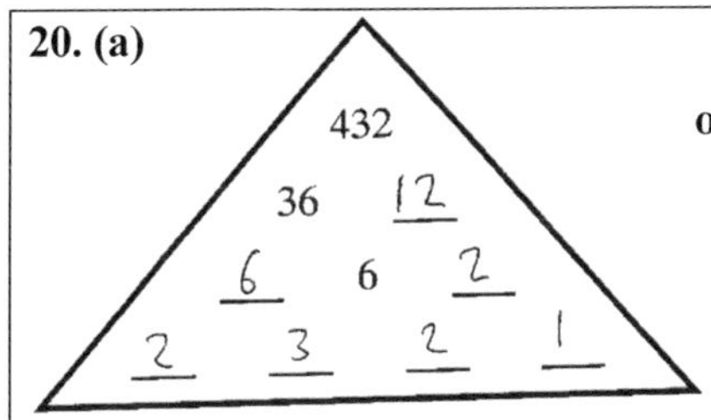

[Triangle: 432, 36, 12, 6, 3, 2, 2, 1, 2, 6, 1] or [Triangle: 432, 36, 12, 6, 6, 2, 1, 1, 2]

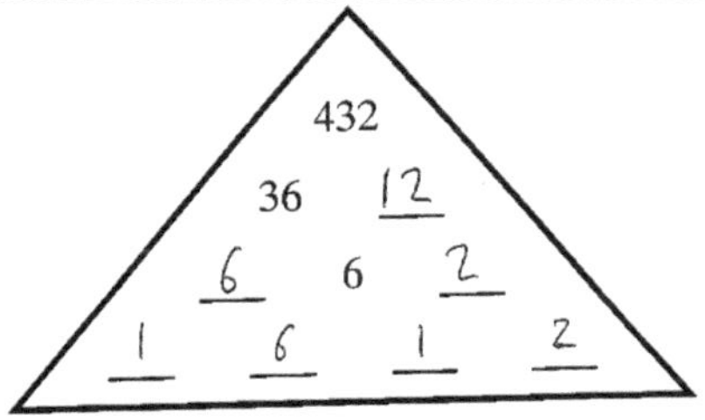

(b)

[Triangle: 4000, 50, 80, 10, 8, 1, 5, 2, 4]

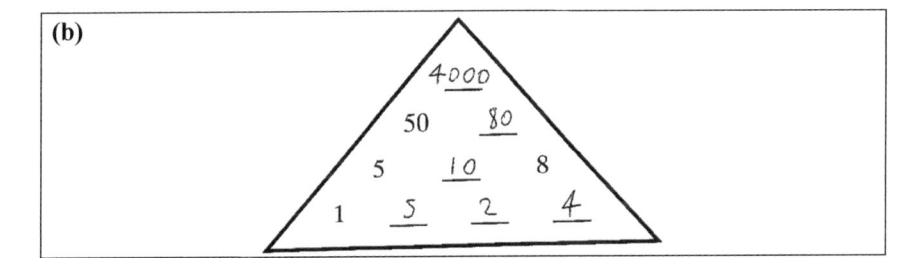

For **(b)**, you need to **begin with the 5 and the 10** ($1 \times 5 = 5$ and $5 \times 10 = 50$). Then you can see that $10 \times 8 = 80$, and so on.

21.

Builders	Time
1000	6 months
1500	4 months

(÷ 2/3 = × 3/2)   (× 2/3)

1500

This very very wordy question includes **an irrelevant piece of information**: that the wall is 154 km long. It is testing your ability not to be confused by this.

- **Start with a table and enter what you know** (1000 builders, 6 months).
- **Add the 4 months** in the next row.
- **What multiple of 6 gives 4?** Answer: $\times \frac{2}{3}$
- If they want to do it more quickly, they need more builders, so you must do the opposite of the multiple: you need to divide by $\frac{2}{3}$.
- $\div \frac{2}{3} = \times \frac{3}{2}$

(b)
- $1000 \times \frac{3}{2} = 500 \times 3 = 1500$

Once you have worked out that **Alec and Nicola together** do the same work as **1 builder**, you need to use the same method as in **(a)**.

'**6000 months**' would probably also be an acceptable answer.

Alec: $\frac{1}{3}$ of a builder
Nicola: $\frac{1}{6} \times 2 = \frac{2}{6} = \frac{1}{3}$ of a builder } Together: 1 builder

Builders	Time
$\frac{1}{1000}$	1 (6 months)
1	500 years

$\frac{1}{1000} \} \times 1000$

22. (a)
$\underline{\underline{900\,m}}$

(b)
$\underline{\underline{0-2 \text{ minutes}}}$

If your answer to **(b)** is wrong but includes or overlaps with the correct time period, it might receive 1 mark.

(c) *Stephanie runs 500m in 2 minutes, then slows down and runs 400m in 3 minutes.*

An answer which contains **most but not all** of this information should still get the marks.

(d) (i)
$\underline{\underline{\dfrac{900}{5} = 180 \text{ m/min}}}$

Average speed $= \dfrac{total\ distance}{total\ time}$ (see **Question 14 (b)** above).

(ii)
$10 - 2 = 8$ mins $\dfrac{900}{8} = \dfrac{450}{4} = \dfrac{225}{2} = \underline{\underline{112.5 \text{ m/min}}}$

The *total* time is 10 minutes (15 − 5), but you need to **remove the 2 minutes when Stephanie stops** to eat chips.

23.
(a) 100 −7 93 −6 87 −5 82 −4 78 −3 75
(b) 5   +2 7   +4 11 +8 19 +16 35 +32 67
(c) 216   125   64   27   8   1
    6^3 5^3 4^3 3^3 2^3 1^3

- You need to get used to **writing the differences between numbers** in a sequence.
- However, you should first **check for square and cube numbers**.

24.

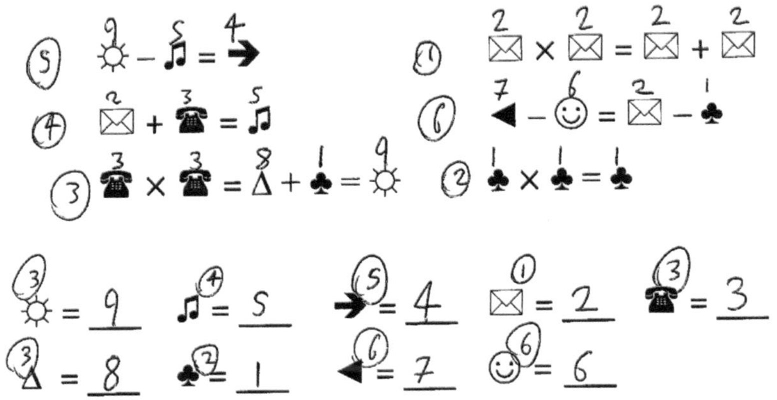

[Puzzle grid with symbols and numbers:]

⑤ ☼ − ♪ = 4
④ ⊠ + ♪ = ♫
③ 📯 × 📯 = △ + ♣ = ☼
     2 × ⊠ = ⊠ + ⊠
     ▼ − ☺ = ♣
     ⊠ − ♣ = ♣

③ ☼ = 9   ④ ♪ = 5   ⑤ ↑ = 4
③ △ = 8   ② ♣ = 1   ⑥ ▼ = 7
① ⊠ = 2   ⑥ ☺ = 6   ③ 📯 = 3

There are different ways of doing this. In the example, I have numbered my steps 1 – 6.

1. This can only be 2.
2. This can only be 1.
3. Apart from 1 and 2, which have already been found, the only number which gives a 1 digit solution when multiplied by itself is 3.
4. Complete this with the numbers you have found already.
5. Complete this with the numbers you have found already.
6. 7 and 6 are the only remaining numbers.

END

Paper 5: *Mr Biggles*

Advanced Level

Papers 5 and 6 are very challenging, requiring a wide range of mathematical skills and the ability to think creatively when presented with unusual, sometimes complex questions. Very few schools set exams which are consistently at this level, but many include a handful of similarly difficult questions towards the end of a paper.

The more complex algebra tasks are unlikely in any 11+ exam, but advanced students would do well to be prepared for such questions.

---

1. **(a)** What is $1 + 2 \times 3 \div 4 - 5 + 6$?

    Answer: ……………… (2)

    (b) Add brackets to make the following calculation correct:

    $$2 \times 8 \div 4 + 8 = 20$$

    (3)

---

2. What is $23 \times 24 \times 25$?

    Answer: ……………… (2)

---

3. **(a)** What is $6 + 2.5 \div 0.5$?

    Answer: ……………… (2)

(b) What is $\dfrac{4.22+4.78}{0.3}$?

Answer: .... **(2)**

---

4. Circle two numbers which have the same value:

$\dfrac{21}{4}$ $\qquad$ $5\dfrac{2}{25}$ $\qquad$ 5.1 $\qquad$ 5.08 $\qquad$ $5\dfrac{1}{11}$

(2)

---

5. Write down the 4 prime numbers which multiply to make 220.

Answer: .... **(2)**

---

6. Two whole numbers between 30 and 40 have a product of 1287.

What are they?

Answer: .... and .... **(2)**

7. How many amounts between 50p and 60p <u>cannot</u> be made with exactly 4 coins?

Answer: .... (2)

8. A group of foxes and wolves (360 in total) were asked whether they preferred to eat lambs or children.

- 64% of the wolves preferred lambs.
- $\frac{7}{12}$ of the animals surveyed were foxes.
- 74 animals preferred children.

Complete the following table, writing the correct number of animals in each box:

	Foxes	Wolves
Prefer Lambs		
Prefer Children		

(4)

9. Two of the following ranges include <u>2 prime numbers, 1 square number and a cube number</u> (a single number might do more than one job).

Circle the two ranges to which this applies.

1-10   11-20   21-30   31-40   41-50

51-60   61-70   71-80   81-90   91-100

(2)

10. Write the missing digits in the boxes:

(a) ☐ 4 ☐ + 5 ☐ 5 = 8 1 1

(b) 5 0 5 2 ÷ ☐ = ☐ 4 2

(c) ☐ 0 4 × 6 ☐ = 3 2 ☐ ☐ 6   **(6)**

11.

$$A + 2B + C = 29$$
$$2B + 2C = 22$$
$$A + B + 2C = 34$$

Find the values of A, B and C.

A: ………   B: ………   C: ………   **(4)**

---

12. Fill in the gaps in the following net, so that it could be folded to make a regular die:

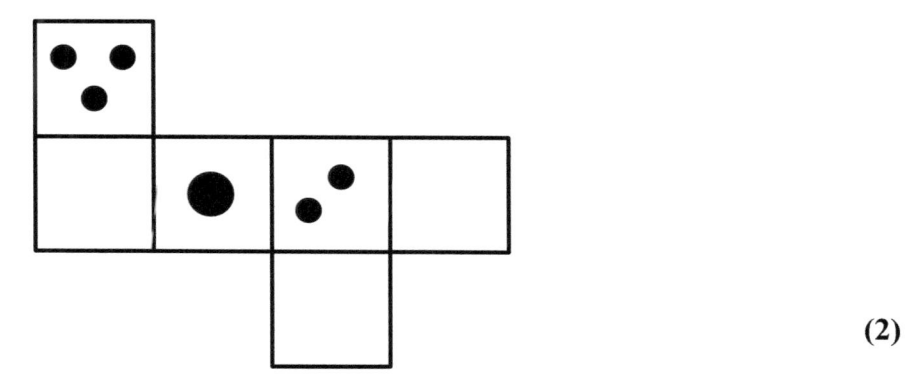

(2)

13. Roderick has 8 fewer T-shirts than Bess. Together they have 22 T-shirts.

How many T-shirts does Bess have?

Answer: ……………… **(2)**

14. The following table shows the first four numbers in three sequences, A, B and C:

	A	B	C
Row 1	1	2	3
Row 2	5	6	7
Row 3	9	10	11
Row 4	13	14	15

In which row and column would the following numbers appear?

(a) 306

Row: …… Column: …… **(2)**

(b) 107

Row: …… Column: …… **(2)**

(c) 2633

Row: …… Column: …… **(2)**

15. Triangle ABC has these measurements:

- AB is 7 cm long
- Angle BAC is 50°
- Angle ABC is greater than 45°
- BC is 6 cm long

A

(a) Complete triangle ABC. **(3)**

(b) What is the length of AC?   Answer: ……………… **(2)**

---

16. Five gorillas weigh a total of 426 kg. Nikki weighs 43 kg more than Natasha and 70 kg more than Giacomo. Alec weighs 38 kg less than Natasha and 146 kg less than Mr Biggles.

How much does each gorilla weigh?

Nikki: ……… kg   Natasha: ……… kg   Giacomo: ……… kg

Alec: ……… kg   Mr Biggles: ……… kg   **(4)**

17. Nicholas has a collection of red, yellow and blue Smarties. He counts them into various groups. The total number of red Smarties and yellow Smarties is 50. The total number of yellow Smarties and blue Smarties is 43. The total number of red Smarties and blue Smarties is 37.

   (a) How many Smarties does Nicholas have in total?

   Answer: ……………… (3)

   (b) How many red Smarties does Nicholas have?

   Answer: ……………… (3)

---

18. Horses use a special kind of maths based on the symbol ₦.

   - 4 ₦ 7 means add 4 to the product of 4 and 7:
     - 4 ₦ 7 = 4 × 7 + 4 = 32
     - 5 ₦ 10 = 5 × 10 + 5 = 55

   (a) (i) What is -5 ₦ 5 ?

   Answer: ……………… (2)

   (ii) What is 3 ₦ -11 ?

   Answer: ……………… (2)

(iii) What is -20 ₦ -3 ?

Answer: ……………… **(2)**

(b) What is 3 ₦ (4 ₦ 5) ?

Answer: ……………… **(2)**

(c) What is Q, if (Q ₦ 8) ₦ 4 = -108 ?

Answer: ……………… **(3)**

19.
- 3 jars of jam and 2 jars of honey cost £4.88.
- 3 jars of honey and 2 jars of jam cost £5.32.

How much does a jar of jam cost?

Answer: ……………… **(4)**

20. Mahalia, the school cook at Gout Hill Primary, is unhappy about the students' diet. She instructs all 120 students to open their lockers and show her how many bags of crisps they are hiding.

She records the results in a frequency table:

Number of bags	0	1	2	3	4	5	6	7	8
Frequency	1	21	16	10	0	0		31	9

(a) Mahalia forgets to complete her frequency table. How many students are hiding 6 bags of crisps?

Answer: .... **(2)**

(b) What is the mean number of crisp bags hidden by each student?

Answer: .... **(3)**

(c) Students with more than 5 bags of crisps are sent home.

(i) What is the percentage change in the number of students at Gout Hill?

Answer: .... **(3)**

(ii) What is the median number of crisp bags belonging to the students who remain at school?

Answer: .... **(2)**

21. Complete the following sequences:

(a) 1   2   2   4   8   32   ___   ___

(b) 2   9   28   65   ___   ___

(c) 1   2   4   4   7   6   10   8   ___   ___   **(6)**

---

22. The blue monsters of Belualand use cookies instead of money. Each kind of cookie has a fixed value.

Here are some calculations using Beluish cookies:

[chocolate chip cookie] × [chocolate chip cookie] = [chocolate chip cookie] + [doughnut] + [doughnut]

[chocolate chip cookie] + [star cookie] = [flower cookie] + [flower cookie]

[flower cookie] + [star cookie] = [striped cookie] + [doughnut]

Solve these problems, drawing **only one** cookie in each box:

[striped cookie] − [chocolate chip cookie] = ☐

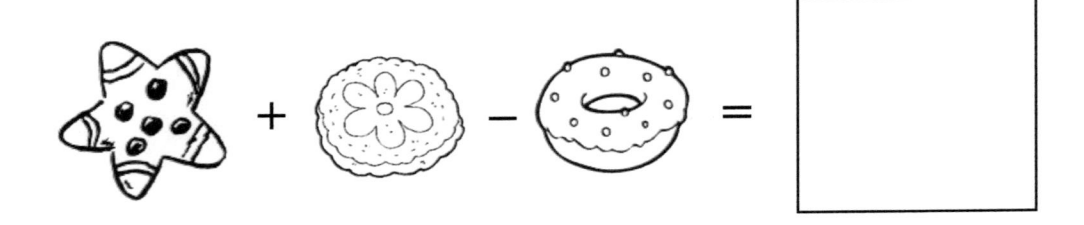

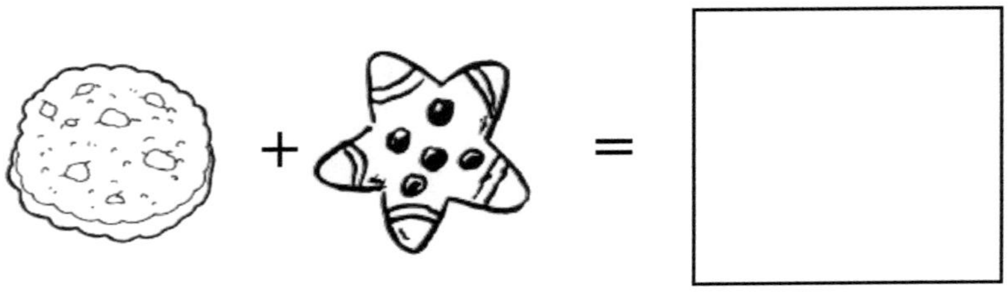

★ + ✿ − ◎ = ▢

◉ + ★ = ▢

(6)

23. I think of a number. I subtract 27 from it then multiply the result by 3. Finally I add 1. The result is a third of my original number.

What was my original number?

Answer: .... **(3)**

TOTAL MARKS: 100

Paper 5: *Mr Biggles*
Solutions

1. (a)

$$1 + 2 \times 3 \div 4 - 5 + 6 = 1 + \underline{6 \div 4} - 5 + 6$$
$$= 1 + \underline{1.5 - 5} + 6 = \underline{2.5 - 5} + 6$$
$$= \underline{-2.5 + 6} = \underline{\underline{3.5}}$$

Remember **BIDMAS**, which tells you the correct order for performing mathematical operations:

- **Brackets**
- **Indices** (e.g. 3^2)
- **Division** and **Multiplication** in order from left to right: division does not need to come first
- **Addition** and **Subtraction** in order from left to right: addition does not need to come first

In each stage of the example, I have underlined the operation that I will perform next.

(b)

$$2 \times (8 \div 4 + 8) = 20$$

If you also put brackets around $8 \div 4$ (which is unnecessary, because the division must happen before the addition anyway), you are likely still to get the marks.

2.

```
    2 3
  × 2 4
  ─────
    9 2
  4 6 0
  ─────
  5 5 2
```

```
    5 5 2
  ×   2 5
  ───────
  2 7 6 0
  1 1 0 4 0
  ─────────
  1 3 8 0 0
```

$$\underline{\underline{13800}}$$

3. (a)

$$6 + 2.5 \div 0.5 = 6 + \frac{2.5}{0.5} = 6 + \frac{25}{5} = 6 + 5 = \underline{\underline{11}}$$

(b)

$$\frac{4.22 + 4.78}{0.3} = \frac{9}{0.3} = \frac{90}{3} = \underline{\underline{30}}$$

In both these answers, notice the method for removing decimals in a fraction: multiplying the top and bottom by 10 (or 100, for 2 decimal places).

4.

$$\frac{21}{4}$$
$$= 5\tfrac{1}{4} = 5.25$$

$\boxed{5\tfrac{2}{25}}$ 5.1 $\boxed{5.08}$ $5\tfrac{1}{11}$

The numbers are easiest to compare if you convert them to decimals.

- Because the answer was found early in the solution, it was unnecessary to convert $5\tfrac{1}{11}$ into a decimal. However, it might also be obvious that this will not produce a neat decimal like the others, and so cannot be one of the answers.

5.

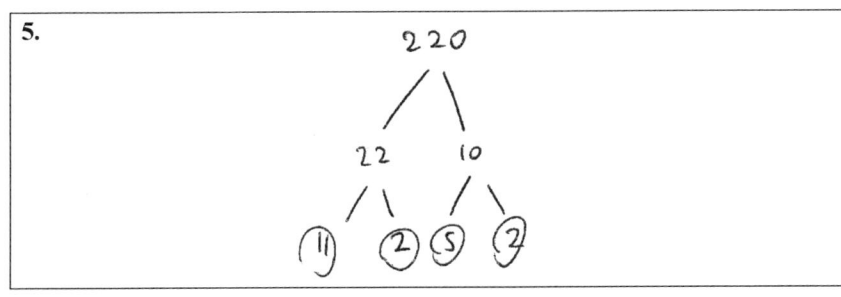

```
      220
     /   \
    22    10
   /  \  /  \
  (11)(2)(5)(2)
```

The first step in a factor tree is to find **any two numbers which multiply to make the original number** (here, 22 and 10). Any other pair, such as 110 and 2, would also lead to the same answers.

Circle prime numbers as you find them.

6.

30 31 32 33 34 35 36 37 38 39 40

Not even. ✓
Not a multiple of 5. ✓

Multiple of 3? $3\overline{)1287}$ = 429   YES

$\dfrac{1287}{33} = \dfrac{429}{11} = \dfrac{39}{11}$; $11\overline{)429}$ = 39 ; $\dfrac{39}{} = 33$

List the numbers.
- 1287 is **odd**, so **neither factor can be even**. (Cross out the even numbers.)
- 1287 **is not a multiple of 5**. (Cross out 35.)

- It **is a multiple of 3**, so at least one of the factors must be a multiple of 3. (Try dividing by 33 then 39.)
- $1287 \div 33 = 39$, so **33 and 39 are the solutions**.

7.

50p: 20+20+5+5   51p: 20+20+10+1   52p: 20+20+10+2
53p: 50+1+1+1   54p: 50+2+1+1   55p: 50+2+2+1   56p: 50+5+2+2
57p: 50+5+1+1   58p: 50+5+2+1   59p: 50+5+2+2
60p: 20+20+10+10   None! ⓪

8.

```
    150
  × 0.64  ⑤
  ─────
    600
   9000
  ─────
   96.00
```

	Prefer Lambs	Foxes	Wolves	
		190 ⑧	96 ⑤	360−74 = 286 ②
	Prefer Children	20 ⑦	54 ⑥	74 ①
$\dfrac{2}{12} \times \dfrac{360}{1} =$		210 ③	150 ④	360

The easiest order in which to complete this question is indicated in the example by numbers in circles.
- You can't begin with the first bullet-point in the question: you need to know how many wolves there are first.
- It is useful to add totals outside the table, as in the example, even though you are not marked for these. Notice the 360 in the bottom-right corner: the totals must themselves add up to this.

9.

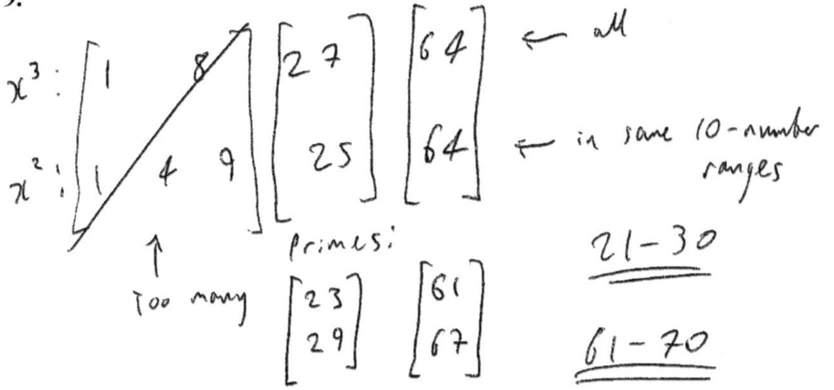

- There aren't many cube numbers between 1 and 100, so the example begins by listing these.

- Next, I list **those square numbers which exist in the same 10-number ranges as the cube numbers**.

- There are too many square and cube numbers in the 1-10 range (the question asks for one of each).

- Therefore the ranges are **21-30** and **61-70**.

In the example I check that there are two prime numbers in each of these ranges, but this is not strictly necessary unless I have made a mistake.

x^3: 1   8   27   64 ← all

x^2: 1   4   9   [25]   [64] ← in same 10-number ranges

↑ too many

primes: [23, 29]   [61, 67]

21-30
61-70

10.

(a) $2\;4\;\boxed{6}\;+\;5\;\boxed{6}\;5\;=\;8\;1\;1$

(b) $5\;0\;5\;2\;\div\;\boxed{6}\;=\;\boxed{8}\;4\;2$

(c) $5\;0\;4\;\times\;6\;\boxed{4}\;=\;32\;\boxed{2}\;\boxed{5}\;6$

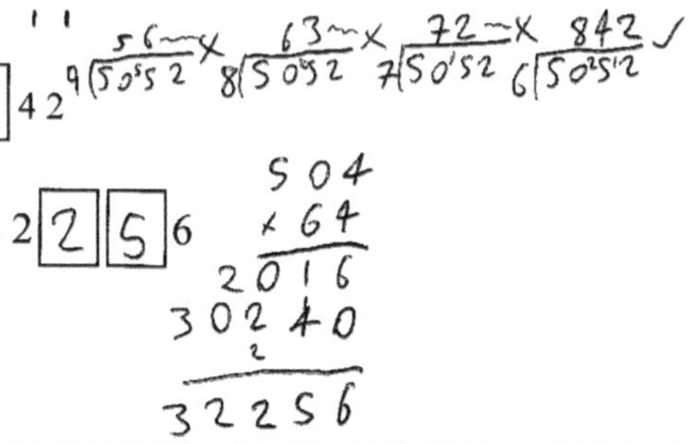

(a) It might be easier to re-write this as a column multiplication; the method, however, is the same.

(b) 5052 **must be divided by more than 5** to give a 3-digit answer; therefore you need to **try dividing by numbers from 6 to 9**.

- You can abandon a division as soon as it obviously is not going to give the correct answer.

(c) This needs a more cunning approach:

- **To give a number beginning with 3**, 6 must be multiplied by 5, so this goes in the first box.

- 4 must be multiplied by 4 or 9 **to give a number ending in 6**. Try 4 first.

- **Work out 504 × 64**. The answer fits in the boxes.

11.
$A + 2B + C = 29$
$2B + 2C = 22$
$A + B + 2C = 34$

$2B + 2C = 22$ (Eleanor)
$B + C = 11$

$A + 2B + C = 29$ (Eleanor)
$A + B + (B + C) = 29$
(Eleanor) $A + B = 18$

$A + B + 2C = 34$
$18 + 2C = 34$
$2C = 16$
$C = 8$

$B + C = 11$
$B + 8 = 11$
$B = 3$

$A + B = 18$
$A + 3 = 18$
$A = 15$

$A = 15$
$B = 3$
$C = 8$

Check: $A + 2B + C = 15 + 2(3) + 8 = 15 + 6 + 8 = 29$ ✓

Note that such a question is extremely rare at 11+, and would only be set by the very most demanding of independent schools.

There are several possible ways of working your way through this question using algebra – and trial and error might also work (though it could take a very long time).

However, the clearest way in is to notice that **because 2B + 2C = 22, B + C must equal 11**.

- You can then **replace B + C with 11** wherever these letters occur in the other equations.
- This will allow you to find that **A + B = 18**.
- By **replacing A + B with 18 in the third equation** you can find that **C is 8.**

From this point, the rest should fall into place.

12.

4 is left over

Opposite faces add up to 7 (see **Paper 3 Q20**).

(You could write numbers instead of drawing dots.)

13.

22 total

If they had the same, 11 each
A has 8 fewer. $\frac{8}{2} = 4$
$11 - 4 = 7$ (Roderick)
$11 + 4 = 15$ (Bess)   15

or

$B + (B - 8) = 22$
         ↑
      Roderick
↑
Bess

$2B - 8 = 22$
$2B = 30$
$B = 15$

14.

A	4n−3	B	4n−2	C	4n−1
1		2		3	
5		6		7	
9		10		11	
13		14		15	

(with +4 between consecutive rows in each column; and 4n, 4n−3, 4n−2, 4n−1 circled as the column formulas; extra column shown: 4n → 4, 8, 12, 16)

Columns **A**, **B** and **C** each form a sequence close to the 4 times table (4, 8, 12 etc.), which could also be called **4n**. **A**, for example, is 3 less than the 4 times table (**4n − 3**).

For each of parts (a), (b) and (c), you need to work out whether the number is in the sequence **4n − 3** (column **A**), **4n − 2** (column **B**), or **4n − 1** (column **C**), then form a simple equation to find out which row it is in.

(a) 306 is even ; must be 4n−2

$4n-2 = 306$
$4n = 308$
$n = \dfrac{308}{4} = \dfrac{154}{2} = 77$

Row **77** Column **B**

(b) 107 is odd.

Try 4n−3: $4n-3 = 107$
$4n = 110$
$n = \dfrac{110}{4}$ ✗ (not a whole number)

Try 4n−1: $4n-1 = 107$
$4n = 108$
$n = \dfrac{108}{4} = \dfrac{54}{2} = 27$

Row **27** Column **C**

(c) 2633 is odd.

Try 4n−3: $4n-3 = 2633$
$4n = 2636$
$n = \dfrac{2636}{4} = 659$

Row **659** Column **A**

---

15. (a)

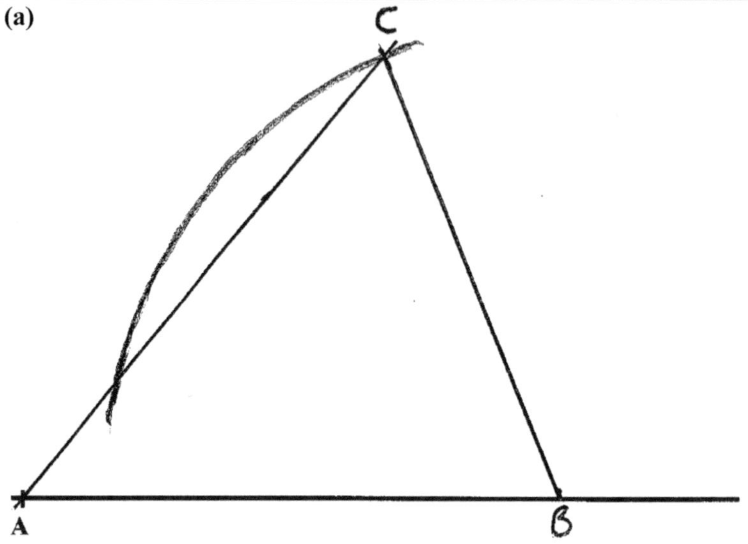

- Draw **AB** along the base.
- '**BAC**' means the angle at **A** (the middle letter). Put a mark on the page at the edge of your protractor to show where 50° lies, then use your ruler to draw a long line from **A**, through your mark, extending further than is likely to be needed.
- **BC** is 6 cm long, but **you don't know in which direction it will point** because you do not know angle **ABC**. Take **a pair of compasses**, extend them to exactly 6 cm along the edge of your ruler, then place the point on **B**. Draw an arc (or arcs) to **show the two places where the arc cuts the line AC**.
- Only one of these points makes **an angle greater than 45°** at **B**.
- Draw a line from **B** to this point.

You will lose marks for inaccuracy, so be very careful at every stage. Check and re-check your measurements.

Lengths in the example answer may be slightly inaccurate, owing to printing adjustments.

(b)

7.3 cm
73 mm

You are likely to get away with an inaccuracy of 1-2 mm in either direction. More than that, and you might lose a mark.

16.

	Alec	Giacomo	Nolesha	Nikki	Mr B.	Total
	54	65	92	135	200 (f guess)	= 546 ↓ −120
−24 from each	30	41	68	111	176	= 426 ← what we want

24
5)120

The best starting point is to **guess a sensible weight for one of the gorillas**.

- I guessed 200 kg for Mr Biggles, then worked out the other weights based on this and wrote them in the table.
- This gave **a total of 546 kg**, which is **120 kg more than the actual total**.
- $120 \div 5 = 24$, so I needed to **subtract 24 from each of the weights** in my guess.

You could also solve this question using algebra. This would not too difficult, but the working would be quite long and fiddly.

---

17. (a)

$R + Y = 50$
$B + Y = 43$
$B + R = 37$
$2B + 2Y + 2R = 130$
$B + Y + R = \underline{\underline{65}}$

If you plunge straight in by working out the number of each kind of Smartie, you will waste time unnecessarily.

(b)

$B + Y + R = 65$
$\underbrace{B+Y} = 43$ (from (A))

$43 + R = 65$
$R = 65 - 43 = \underline{\underline{22}}$

Other algebraic methods would also work, but this is by far the simplest.

18. (a) (i)

$(-5) \times 5 + (-5) = -25 - 5 = \underline{-30}$

(ii)

$3 \times (-11) + 3 = -33 + 3 = \underline{-30}$

(iii)

$(-20) \times (-3) + (-20) = 60 - 20 = \underline{40}$

(b)

$3 ₦ (4 \times 5 + 4) = 3 ₦ (24)$

$= 3 \times 24 + 3 = 72 + 3 = \underline{75}$

(c)

$-108 = (Q ₦ 8) ₦ 4 = (Q \times 8 + Q) ₦ 4 = (8Q + Q) ₦ 4 = 9Q ₦ 4$

$= 9Q \times 4 + 9Q = 36Q + 9Q = 45Q$

$45Q = -108$

$Q = -\frac{108}{45} = \underline{-2.4}$

In **(b)** and **(c)**, notice how the answer is built up step by step, dealing with one **₦** at a time.

*As well as being used by horses, **₦** is a symbol for the Nigerian currency, the Naira.*

19.

$3J + 2H = 488 \rightarrow (\times 3)\ 9J + 6H = 1464$

$2J + 3H = 532 \rightarrow (\times 2)\ 4J + 6H = 1064$

$(-)\ 5J = 400$

$J = \underline{80p}$

You can multiply each equation by a different amount, so long **as everything within a single equation** is multiplied by the same amount. This way you make equations with **the same number of H**, so that you can **subtract them** and **eliminate this variable.**

- You subtract (or add) equations **to eliminate a variable** (letter), leaving an **equation in one variable** (**5J = 400**), which you can solve.

*If you then wanted to find the price of a jar of honey, you would replace **J** with **80p** in one of the original equations, and solve it to find **H**.*

20. (a)

$120 - (1 + 21 + 15 + 10 + 31 + 10) = 120 - 88 = \underline{32}$

(b)

Total bags: $0 \times 1 + 1 \times 21 + 2 \times 16 + 3 \times 10 + 4 \times 0 + 5 \times 0 + 6 \times 32 + 7 \times 31 + 8 \times 9$

$= 0 + 21 + 32 + 30 + 192 + 217 + 72$

$= 564$

$\frac{\text{Bags}}{\text{Students}} = \frac{564}{120} = \frac{188}{40} = \frac{94}{20} = \frac{47}{10} = \underline{4.7}$

To find the number of bags, you need to **multiply the number of bags** in each column of the table **by the frequency** (how many students have that number of bags).

(c) (i)

$32 + 31 + 9 = 72$ sent home

$$\frac{72}{120} = \frac{36}{60} = \frac{12}{20} = \frac{6}{10} = 60\%$$

I recommend always starting awkward divisions by writing the problem as a fraction and simplifying / reducing. This way you make the problem easier, and sometimes (like in this question) avoid doing a division altogether.

Be careful to find the **percentage *change***, rather than what percentage of the students is left.

(ii)

$120 - 72 = 48$

$\frac{48}{2} = 24$ Median is the '24.5th' student.

Bags	0	1	2	3	4	5
Freq.	11	21	16	10	0	0

← 24.5th student is in this group

Median is 2

There are 48 students remaining; the median is **the middle value** in the group, **counting from smallest to largest**. If you broke 48 into two equal groups, you would have 1-24 and 25-48: the median value would lie half way between the 24th and 25th students.

- Work **from left to right along the frequency row of the table** until you reach **a total of 24.5**.
- As this is **in the '2 bags' column, the median is 2**.

21.

(a) 1   2   4   8   16   32   256   8192
         ×2 ×2 ×2 ×8 ×32 ×256×32

(b) 2   9   28   65   126   217
         ²+1 3³+1 4³+1
         +3   +3   +3

(c) 1   2   4   7   6   10   8   13
         +2   +2   +2   +2
             +3   +3   +3

This is a really horrible sequences question. Sometimes exams are set by people who hate children, in which case you will have to put up with things like this.

The most important piece of advice when faced with a question as irritating as this one is to skip it and come back to it when you have finished everything else: otherwise it might eat up the rest of your time.

However, once you are familiar with the main kinds of sequence at 11+, you have a good chance of spotting the patterns here:

(a) Sometimes sequences develop by **adding together** or **multiplying** the preceding numbers. This is the multiplying kind. The clue hidden in this one is that two numbers near the beginning are the same (because $1 \times 2 = 2$).

(b) If a sequence goes up in **intervals which get bigger very quickly**, it is likely to be based on **square** or **cube numbers**. This sequence is a list of the cube numbers, with 1 added to each.

(c) If some numbers get big while others do not (so that here, 8 comes after 10), you are likely to have **two overlapping sequences**. If this turns up in an exam, both the sequences will be simple ones (here, +2 and +3).

If you got these right, give yourself a pat on the back.

$\begin{array}{r} 72 \\ \times 8 \\ \hline 576 \end{array}$ $\begin{array}{r} 256 \\ \times 32 \\ \hline 512 \\ 7680 \\ \hline 8192 \end{array}$

22.

And now, a more enjoyable question!

So you don't waste half an hour drawing cookies, it is a good idea to **replace them with letters** while you solve the problem:

$$A \times A = A + B + B$$
$$A + C = D + D$$
$$D + C = E + B$$

By far the easiest way forward is to **work out numbers with which the cookies might be replaced**. It is sensible to **start with small numbers**, only moving to larger ones if these don't work.

(Because we are dealing with Beluish money, not British money, there is no reason to assume that the values are 1, 2, 5, 10, 20 etc.)

$A \times A = A + B + B$ If A is 2: $2 \times 2 = 2 + 1 + 1$ ∴ $B = 1$
$A + C = D + D$ $2 + C = D + D$
$D + C = E + B$ (maybe C is 4?
                                    $2 + 4 = 3 + 3$ ∴ D is 3
                                    $3 + 4 = E + 1$ ∴ $E = 6$

Then work is $A = 2$ $B = 1$ $C = 4$ $D = 3$ $E = 6$

$E - A = 6 - 2 = 4 = C$
$C + D - B = 4 + 3 - 1 = 6 = E$
$A + C = 2 + 4 = 6 = E$

So, finally:

- **A** cannot be 1, but (based on the first equation) **B** could be: making **A** worth 2.
- If **A** is 2, **C** cannot be 3 (unless **D** is not a whole number … we don't want that), but it could be 4, which would make **D** worth 3.
- This makes **E** worth 6. It all works!

Now that you have a value for each kind of cookie, you are ready to solve the problems in the question:

23.

$$(N-27) \times 3 + 1 = \frac{N}{3}$$

$$3N - 81 + 1 = \frac{N}{3}$$

$$3N - 80 = \frac{N}{3}$$

$$9N - 240 = N$$

$$9N = N + 240$$

$$8N = 240$$

$$N = \frac{240}{8} = \underline{\underline{30}}$$

or (trial and improvement):

Number	−27	×3	+1	Result is 1/3 of Number?
100	73	219	220	No
50	23	69	70	No
20	−7	−21	−20	No
40	13	39	40	No
30	3	9	10	Yes

END

Paper 6: *Goblins in the Casino Royale*
Advanced Level

1. **(a)** Subtract -8 from -10.

   Answer: ……………… **(2)**

   (b) What is $(-3)^3$?

   Answer: ……………… **(2)**

2. Multiply 563 by 4988.

   Answer: ……………… **(2)**

3. Divide 74912 by 16.

   Answer: ……………… **(2)**

4. What is 5.06×11.8 ?

Answer: .... **(2)**

---

5. What number is exactly half way between 4.22 and 5.7?

Answer: .... **(2)**

---

6. Circle the fractions that are smaller than $\frac{3}{7}$.

$$\frac{1}{3} \qquad \frac{2}{5} \qquad \frac{1}{2} \qquad \frac{4}{9} \qquad \frac{5}{11}$$

(3)

7. A square with side length 3 cm is cut from a triangle. The remaining area of the triangle is 43 cm².

   How long is the length **b**?

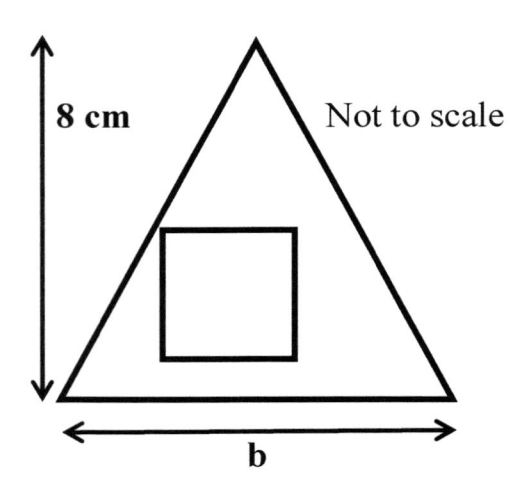

   Answer: ……………… (3)

---

8. (a) $\dfrac{5}{6} \times \dfrac{3}{4} =$

   Answer: ……………… (2)

   (b) $1\dfrac{4}{5} \div 1\dfrac{1}{2} =$

   Answer: ……………… (2)

   (c) $\dfrac{8}{11} - \dfrac{4}{5} =$

   Answer: ……………… (2)

9. How many prime numbers are there between 80 and 100?

Answer: ……………… **(2)**

10. Complete the triangle by writing a different digit from 1 to 9 in each circle. The calculations should work in the direction of the arrows. Two numbers have been entered for you.

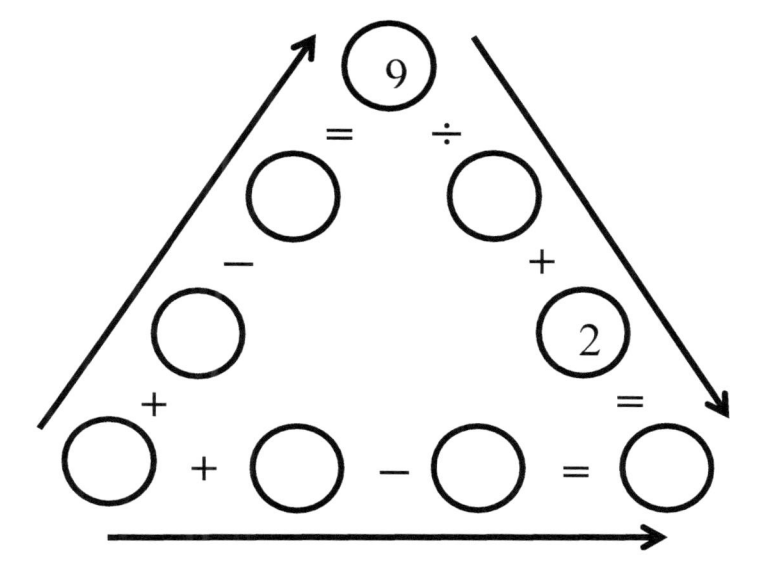

(3)

11. Chris is running the London Marathon, which is 26 miles long. He starts at 10:07 and finishes at 13:35.

(a) For how many hours and minutes does Chris run?

Answer: ……hrs……mins **(2)**

(b) On average, how many minutes does it take Chris to run a mile?

Answer: ……………… **(3)**

12. Baptiste, Timothee and Augustin share out some money so that they each have the same amount. Baptiste gives Augustin £3.80 and Augustin gives Timothee £2.95. They have £12.60 in total.

How much did each of them have before sharing out the money?

Baptiste: .... Timothee: .... Augustin: .... (3)

13. I fill a third of a measuring jug with rice. I tip 100g of rice back into the bag, leaving the jug $\frac{1}{4}$ full.

How much rice can the jug hold when full?

Answer: .... (3)

14. Nora's score in a maths test was 110% of the mean score of the other students in her class.

Here are the marks of the other students:

    5 scored 92%
    8 scored 74%
    3 scored 64%
    4 scored 59%
    4 scored 50%

What percentage did Nora score?

Answer: ……………… (4)

---

15. Each letter in the following word represents a different number from 1 to 7.

G O B L I N S

O represents 4.

$B + O + G = 12$

$B + I + G = 10$

$S + O + B = 13$

(a) What does $B + O + G + S$ equal?

Answer: ……………… (3)

(b) What does $B + I + O + G + S$ equal?

Answer: .... **(2)**

16. In 5 years' time, the combined age of my three grandparents will be 237. The range of their ages is 15 years.

    (a) What was their combined age 7 years ago?

    Answer: .... **(2)**

    (b) What was the range of their ages 10 years ago?

    Answer: .... **(1)**

17. Milla's alarm clock is slow, and loses 4 minutes every 24 hours.

    She sets it to the correct time before she goes to bed on the 2nd of March, at which point it shows this time:

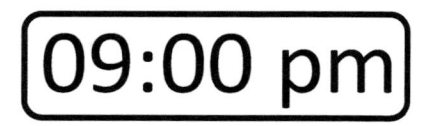

    > 09:00 pm

    (a) When the real time is 9 am on the 7th of March, what time will Milla's clock show?

    Answer: .... **(3)**

(b) If Milla does not adjust her clock, on which date will it next show the correct time?

Answer: ……………… **(4)**

18. **(a)** What is the angle between the minute and hour hands of a clock at 4 o'clock?

Answer: ……………… **(2)**

(b) Find the angle between the hands at 9:30 am.

Answer: ……………… **(3)**

19. **(a)** Fill in the empty boxes in the sequences **Q** and **Q²** below:

Q:	1	2	3		5	
Q²:		4				

(2)

(b) Complete the first numbers in the sequence **Q² + Q** by filling in the empty boxes:

Q² + Q:	2					

(2)

(c) **(i)** Calculate the 100th number in the sequence **T**, which begins like this (you may wish to bear in mind your answer to **(b)**):

T:	-1	3	9	17	27	39

Answer: .... **(4)**

(ii) Work out the missing number in the following sentence (you may need to use <u>trial and improvement</u>):

1479 is the .... th number in sequence T. **(4)**

20. Each row and column in this table adds up to the same amount:

A	30	A	A
15	C	20	B
B	B	16	12
17	5	A	20

Which numbers should replace the letters A, B and C?

A: 6   B: 10   C: 3   (5)

---

21. Louis is practising his driving by doing laps of the Silverstone racing circuit.

The circuit is 6 km long.

Louis drives each lap faster than the previous one, until he completes the final lap in 4 minutes 10 seconds.

(a) What is Louis's average speed on the final lap in km/h? Give your answer as a decimal.

Answer: 86.4 km/h   (4)

(b) Louis increased his average speed by 20% overall, from the first lap to the last. How many minutes did he take to complete the first lap?

Answer: .... **(4)**

---

22. An ordinary pack of playing cards contains 52 cards divided into 4 suits:

Clubs ♣;   Diamonds ♦;   Hearts ♥; Spades ♠

Each suit contains 13 cards. For example, here is the suit of Spades:

In the game of Plonker, you hold 5 cards in your hand, which the other players cannot see. Other cards are picked at random from the pack and placed one at a time on the table. These can be combined with the cards in your hand to make combinations.

For example, three Aces:

… or a straight:

(a) Tilly is practising by herself. She has these cards in her hand:

… and these on the table:

The rest of the cards are in the pack.

(i) What is the probability that the next card to be placed on the table will give her three 4s?

Answer: ……………… **(2)**

(ii) What is the probability that the next card to be placed on the table will give her a straight?

Answer: ……………… **(2)**

(b) Debbie is playing Plonker against Tilly.

Debbie has these cards in her hand:

[A♣, 5♣, 6♣, 8♣, J♥]

Tilly has these cards in her hand:

[A♥, A♠, 2♦, 8♠, 10♥]

These cards are already on the table:

[7♣, 4♦, A♦, K♥]

The rest of the cards are in the pack.

The final card is about to be placed on the table.

- Debbie will definitely win if she completes a <u>straight flush</u>: five cards in a row, **all in the same suit**.
- Tilly will definitely win if she completes a <u>full house</u>: three of one kind of card and two of another.

(i) What is the probability that Debbie will win with a straight flush?

Answer: ……………… (3)

(ii) What is the probability that Tilly will win with a full house?

Answer: ……………… **(4)**

TOTAL MARKS: 100

Paper 6: Goblins in the Casino Royal

Solutions

1. (a) $-(0-(-8)) = -(0+8) = -2$

(b) $(-3)^3 = (-3) \times (-3) \times (-3) = 9 \times (-3) = -27$

2.
```
    4988
  ×  563
  ------
   14964
  299280
 2494000
 -------
 2808244
```
2,808,244

3. $\dfrac{74912}{16} = \dfrac{37456}{8}$

```
   4 6 8 2
 8)3 7⁵4⁵5¹6
```

or

```
   3 7 4 5 6
 2)7⁴4 9¹2
```

```
     4 6 8 2
 16)7 4 9 1 2
     6 4
     ---
     1 0 9
       9 6
     -----
       1 3 1
       1 2 8
       -----
           3 2
```

4682

4.
```
      5.06
    × 1.8  (×3)
    ------
     40 48
    50 60
    ------
    59.708
```
59.708

As the example demonstrates, you can make your division simpler if you are able to reduce your numbers as a fraction before dividing.

The 3 decimal places shared between the numbers in the question mean that you must count back 3 places in your answer.

- When you **multiply** decimals, the decimal points in the question **do not** need to line up.

5.
```
   4.22
 + 5.70
 ------
   9.92
```

```
     4.96
 2)9.9¹2
```
4.96

To find the half way point between two numbers, **find their mean**. In other words:

- Add them together.
- Divide the answer by 2.

6.

$$\frac{3}{7} = \frac{15}{35} = \frac{27}{63} = \frac{33}{77}$$

$$\boxed{\frac{1}{3}} = \frac{3}{9}$$

$$\boxed{\frac{2}{5}} = \frac{14}{35}$$

$$\frac{1}{2}$$

$$\frac{4}{9} = \frac{28}{63}$$

$$\frac{5}{11} = \frac{35}{77}$$

- $\frac{1}{3}$ is $\frac{3}{9}$ and therefore smaller than $\frac{3}{7}$.
- $\frac{2}{5}$ is $\frac{14}{35}$ and therefore smaller than $\frac{3}{7}$, which is equivalent to $\frac{15}{35}$.
- $\frac{1}{2}$ is clearly too large.

The treatment of the last two numbers is similar, as shown in the example.

7.

$3 \times 3 = 9 \text{ cm}^2$

Total area: $43 + 9 = 52 \text{ cm}^2$

Triangle: $\frac{1}{2} \times b \times 8 = 52$

$b \times 4 = 52$

$b = 13 \text{ cm}$

To solve this, you need to know that the area of a triangle is $\frac{1}{2} \times$ **base** $\times$ **height**.

8. (a)

$$\frac{5}{\cancel{6}_2} \times \frac{\cancel{27}^1}{4} = \frac{5}{8}$$

(b)

$$1\frac{4}{5} \div 1\frac{1}{2} = \frac{9}{5} \div \frac{3}{2} = \frac{\cancel{9}^3}{5} \times \frac{2}{\cancel{3}_1} = \frac{6}{5}$$

You could also give your answer to **(b)** as $1\frac{1}{5}$.

(c)

$$\frac{8}{11} - \frac{4}{5} = \frac{40}{55} - \frac{44}{55} = -\frac{4}{55}$$

9. 83, 89, 97

10.

[Triangle diagram 1:]
9 ÷ 3 × 2 = ⓒ
÷
6 + 4 - 1 =
=   =   =
6 + 7 - 8 = ⑤

or

[Triangle diagram 2:]
9 ÷ 3 × 2 = ⓒ
÷
8 + 7 - 6 =
=   =   =
8 + 1 - 4 = ⑤

or

[Triangle diagram 3:]
9 ÷ 3 × 2 = ⓒ
÷
4 + 6 - 1 =
=   =   =
4 + 8 - 7 = ⑤

- The only whole number (apart from 9) by which you can divide 9, to make a different whole number, is 3.
- This gives 5 in the bottom right corner.
- You then need to experiment with numbers in the bottom left corner.

11. (a)

10:07 $\overset{3\,hrs}{\frown}$ 13:07 $\overset{28\,mins}{\frown}$ 13:35   3 hrs 28 mins

When you work with times (which are grouped in 60s and 24s rather than 10s and 100s), number lines are more useful than column arithmetic.

(b)
3 × 60 = 180   180 + 28 = 208 mins $\frac{208}{26} = \frac{104}{13} = 8$ mins

---

12. $\frac{12.60}{3} = £4.20$ each afterwards.

Baptiste: 4.20 + 3.80 = £8   Timothée: 4.20 − 2.95 = £1.25

Augustin: 12.60 − (8 + 1.25) = 12.60 − 9.25 = £3.35

Augustin's situation is complex, because he receives **and** gives money. It is easier to work out what Baptiste and Timothée started with, then find Augustin's amount by subtracting these from the total.

You could use algebra, but this question is simpler without it.

13.

[Diagram: bar split showing ¼, ⅓, 100g labels]
$\frac{1}{3} - \frac{1}{4} = \frac{4}{12} - \frac{3}{12} = \frac{1}{12}$

100 g = $\frac{1}{12}$ of a jug   100 × 12 = 1200 g or 1.2 kg

When a question refers to a physical object (a container, a clock, etc.), it is always helpful to sketch it so that you can label the amounts. This will clarify your working.

- The **difference between a third and a quarter** is a twelfth ($\frac{1}{3} - \frac{1}{4} = \frac{1}{12}$).
- This difference **is also 100g**.
- If $\frac{1}{12}$ is 100g, $\frac{12}{12}$ (a whole) must be **1200g**.

14.

$5 \times 92 = 460$
$8 \times 74 = 592$
$3 \times 64 = 192$
$4 \times 59 = 236$
$4 \times 50 = 200$

$\overline{24} \quad \overline{1680}$

$\dfrac{1680}{24} = \dfrac{840}{12} = \dfrac{420}{6} = \dfrac{210}{3} = 70$

Mean is 70%.

110% of $70 = 1.1 \times 70$

$\begin{array}{r} 70 \\ \times 1.1 \\ \hline 70 \\ 70.0 \\ \hline 77.0 \end{array}$

$\underline{\underline{77\%}}$

Firstly, you need to **find the mean** of the other students' scores:

- **Find the total of their scores** by multiplying the percentages by the frequencies and adding.
- **Divide this by the number of other students**, which is 24.
- The mean is **70%**.

Then **find 110% of 70**.

15.

$\underline{S} = \underline{G} + 1$
$\underline{I} = \underline{O} - 2 = 4 - 2 = 2$ $\underline{I} \underset{3}{2} \cancel{4} \underset{S}{5} \underset{}{6} \underset{O}{7}$

$\underline{G}$ and $\underline{S}$ must be 5 and 6 or 6 and 7

If $\underline{S} = 6$ and $\underline{S} + \underline{O} + \underline{B} = 13$, then $6 + 4 + B = 13$ and $B = 3$

Then $\underline{G} = \underline{S} - 1 = 6 - 1 = 5$

Then $\underline{B} + \underline{O} + \underline{G} = 3 + 4 + 5 = 12$ ✓
$\underline{B} + \underline{I} + \underline{G} = 3 + 2 + 5 = 10$ ✓   Therefore $\underline{S} = 6$ is correct.

$\underline{G} = 5 \quad \underline{O} = 4 \quad \underline{B} = 3 \quad \underline{L} = ? \quad \underline{I} = 2 \quad \underline{N} = ? \quad \underline{S} = 6$

(a) $3 + 4 + 5 + 6 = \underline{\underline{18}}$ **(b)** $18 + 2 = \underline{\underline{20}}$

OR ... see below

In the example, the letters are underlined to avoid confusion with numbers.

There are other ways into this question, and **any approach is likely to involve a degree of trial and error**. The example keeps this to a minimum:

- **I** can be calculated because the different between **BOG** and **BIG** is 2 and we know that **O** is 4.
- **G** and **S** are **consecutive** (because B + O + S [SOB] is worth 1 more than B + O + G), so they can only be 5 and 6 or 6 and 7: 2 and 4 have been found, so no other consecutive numbers between 1 and 7 are available.
- From this point, the two possibilities for **G** and **S** are tried (in the example, the first attempt is successful).
- **B** is now known.

The values of **L** and **N** cannot be worked out, but they are not needed for questions **(a)** and **(b)**.

BUT what if you tried 6 and 7 instead of 5 and 6, for the values of **G** and **S**?
This would give the following: **G** = 6, **O** = 4, **B** = 2, **I** = 2, **S** = 7
Therefore **BOGS** = 17 and **BIOGS** = 19. **There are two possible solutions!**

16. (a)

$$7 + 5 = 12 \quad 12 \times 3 = 36 \quad 237 - 36 = 201$$

The difference between 5 years' time and 7 years ago is 12 years. In other words, 7 years ago **each grandparent was 12 years younger** than they will be in 5 years' time. 12 × 3 is 36.

(b)

15 years

In a sense, this is a trick question: because people get older or younger at the same rate, **the range of their ages does not change**.

---

17. (a)

4.5 days   4.5 × 4 = 18 minutes

9 am − 18 mins = 08:42 am

The clock loses 4 minutes every 24 hours (each day).

9 am on the 7th is 4 days and 12 hours (4.5 days) in the future.

(b)

Needs to be 24 hrs slow

24 × 60 = 1440 mins
```
  24
 ×60
────
1440
```

$$4\overline{)1440} \to 360$$

It will take 360 days.

2nd of March − 5 days   365 days in a year.
= 25th of February

- The clock will next show the correct time **when it is 24 hours slow**.
- 24 hours is 1440 minutes.
- If it loses 4 minutes a day, the clock will take **360 days** to show the correct time again.

Rather than counting forwards 360 days, it is much simpler to **count backwards**.

- There are **365 days in a normal year**, so **count backwards 5 days** (remembering that February has 28 days).
- (Or you could count backwards 6 days including the 29th of February, if for some reason you are a fan of leap years!)

---

18. (a)

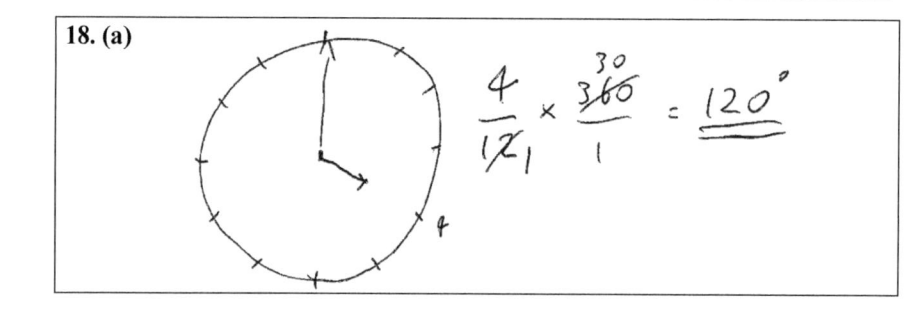

$$\frac{4}{12_1} \times \frac{\cancel{360}^{30}}{1} = 120°$$

(b)

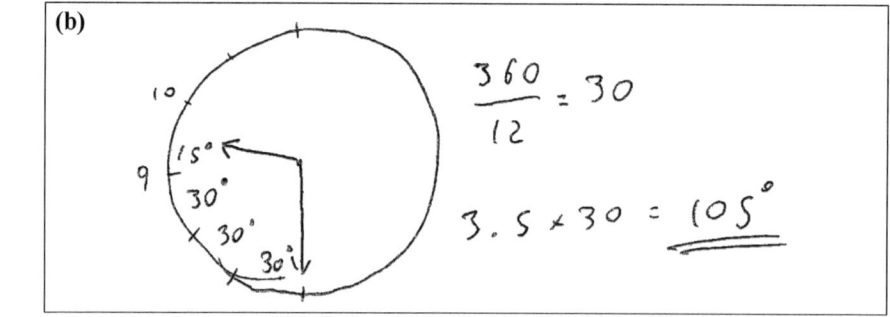

$$\frac{360}{12} = 30$$

3.5 × 30 = 105°

Part **(b)** is testing your ability to remember that **the hour hand will be half way between 9 and 10**, so the total is **90° plus 15°**.

Always do a rough sketch of a clock face for time questions – it will help you to avoid mistakes.

This question is simpler than it looks if you think about it logically.

19. (a)

Q:	1	2	3	4	5	6
Q²:	1	4	9	16	25	36

(b)

| Q² + Q: | 2 | 6 | 12 | 20 | 30 | 42 |

(b) simply involves adding together the rows from (a).

(c) (i)

| T: | -1 | 3 | 9 | 17 | 27 | 39 |

2−3 6−3 12−3 20−3 30−3 42−3

$T = Q^2 + Q - 3$ $100^2 + 100 - 3$
                  $= 10000 + 97 = 10097$

Each of the rows in T is **3 less than** in Q² + Q. Therefore the formula for T must be Q² + Q − 3. **Replace Q with 100** to find the answer.

(ii)

$1479 = Q^2 + Q - 3$

Q	Q²	Q² + Q − 3
20	400	417
30	900	927
40	1600	1637
35	1225	1257
37	1369	1403
⓷⓼	1444	1479

 35
×35

 175
1050

1225

 37
×37

 259
1110

1369

 38
×38

 304
1140

1444

38

To solve this equation you will probably need to use **trial and improvement**.

A clear table for your working makes a huge difference.

- This way your trial and improvement results won't become mixed up with your other working out, such as the multiplications in the example.

20.

$3A + 30 = 17 + 5 + A + 20$
$3A + 30 = 42 + A$
$3A - A = 42 - 30$
$2A = 12$
$\underline{A = 6}$

$3A + 30 = 3 \times 6 + 30 = 48$ in each row/column

$B + B + (6 + (2 = 48 \qquad 15 + C + 20 + B = 48$
$2B + 28 = 48 \qquad\qquad B = 10$
$2B = 20 \qquad\qquad 15 + C + 20 + 10 = 48$
$\underline{B = 10} \qquad\qquad C + 45 = 48$
$\qquad\qquad\qquad\qquad \underline{C = 3}$

You could approach this question from various directions, but this is the simplest:

- Take **two rows/columns which only include one letter (A)**, which is the first and fourth rows, which only include **A**).
- Because they **add up to the same number**, you can use them to **form an equation**.
- **Solve the equation** to find the value of the letter (**A**), which is 6.
- Now **find the total value of a row/column**, by replacing A with 6 in each case: for example, using the top row, $6 + 30 + 6 + 6 = \mathbf{48}$.

Now you can work your way around the grid to find **B** and **C**.

---

21. (a)

$\dfrac{6}{4\frac{1}{6}} = \dfrac{36}{25}$

$\begin{array}{r} 1.44 \\ 25\overline{)36.00} \\ \underline{25} \\ 110 \\ \underline{100} \\ 100 \\ \underline{100} \\ 0 \end{array}$

$= 1.44$ km/min

60 mins in an hour

$\begin{array}{r} 1.44 \\ \times60 \\ \hline 86.40 \end{array}$

$\underline{86.4 \text{ km/h}}$

- $Speed = \dfrac{Distance}{Time}$.
- **The time is not 4.10**, because 10 seconds is not 0.10 of a minute.
- It is best to **use a fraction** ($4\frac{1}{6}$), because the decimal is fiddly (4.166666…) and what's more would need to be rounded to 4.167, making your answer inaccurate.
- Simplify the calculation by **multiplying top and bottom by 6, then divide 36 by 25**. This gives a speed in **km per minute**.
- **Multiply this by 60** to give Louis's speed in **km per hour**.

(b)

Lap $\xrightarrow{\times 1.2}$ Lap 4
$\div 1.2 \quad 86.4$ km/h
72 km/h

$T = \dfrac{D}{S} = \dfrac{6}{72} = \dfrac{2}{24} = \dfrac{1}{12} \text{ h} \quad \dfrac{60}{12} = 5 \text{ minutes}$

$\dfrac{864}{1.2} = \dfrac{864}{12} = \dfrac{432}{6} = \dfrac{216}{3} = 72$

If Louis increased his average speed by 20%, **his original speed would be multiplied by 1.2 to give his final speed**: to reverse this, *divide his final speed by 1.2*.

- *You **cannot** solve this by finding 80% of his final speed* (see **Paper 4 Q9**).

When you have his original speed (72 km per hour), you can use the equation $Time = \frac{Distance}{Speed}$ to find **how much time the lap took** in hours.

Finally, you need **to convert this into minutes**.

(*You know **the percentage by which his speed, not his time, changed**. Therefore you need to find his first lap speed, **then** work out his time. If you try to convert his final lap time directly into his first lap time without working out the different speeds, you are likely to make a mess of things.*)

22. (a) (i)

$52 - 7 = 45$ in the pack

$\frac{2}{45}$

The maths in Question 22 is not in itself difficult. The challenge is to absorb a large amount of information, so that you understand what is relevant and how to apply it.

In this question:

- There are 5 cards in Tilly's hand and 2 on the table, so there are **45 left in the pack**.
- She needs a number 4, and there are 2 of these somewhere in the pack.

(ii)

Any [5] $\frac{4}{45}$

The example in the question, above part **(a)**, makes clear that a **straight** is formed of **5 consecutive cards from any suits**, so any number 5 will work for Tilly.

- Tilly would make a straight by combining the 7 on the table with the 4, 6 and 8 in her hand, then turning over a 5 to fill the gap in the sequence.

(b) (i)

$52 - 14 = 38$ $\frac{2}{38} = \frac{1}{19}$

- There are **38 cards left in the pack**.
- Debbie needs a **4 of clubs** or a **9 of clubs**.

Remember to simplify your answer, or you will lose a mark.

(ii)

She already has 3 Aces.

Hand: Another 2: $\frac{3}{38}$ Another 8: $\frac{2}{38}$ Another 10: $\frac{3}{38}$

Table: Another 7: $\frac{3}{38}$ Another 4: $\frac{3}{38}$ Another King: $\frac{3}{38}$

$\frac{3}{38} + \frac{2}{38} + \frac{3}{38} + \frac{3}{38} + \frac{3}{38} + \frac{3}{38} = \frac{17}{38}$

Tilly already has 3 Aces (she can't get 4, because Debbie has the other one), so she needs **two of any other kind of card**.

Looking at the cards in her hand:

- There are 3 more number 2 cards in the pack.
- There are **2 more** number 8 cards, **because Debbie has one in her hand**.
- There are 3 more number 10 cards.

But Tilly could also get a double **if one of the cards on the table is repeated**:

- There are 3 more 7s, 4s and Kings in the pack.

Adding the probabilities together gives $\frac{17}{38}$.

END

RESOURCES TO PRINT AND KEEP

RSL EDUCATIONAL'S ALL-IN-ONE HOME 11-PLUS SERVICE

SUPPORTING YOU ALL THE WAY TO THE EXAM

INDIVIDUAL FEEDBACK AVAILABLE

11 PLUS LIFELINE

WWW.11PLUSLIFELINE.COM

ONE MONTHLY FEE
NO PAYMENT CONTRACT

11 Plus Lifeline is the all-round solution for your child's 11+ preparation. It's also perfect for any child who wants an engaging, enjoyable way to reinforce their Key Stage 2 knowledge.

- Challenging, original practice papers to download and print.
- Fully worked example answers for every question, with step-by-step explanations: like expert private tuition.
- Suitable for independent and grammar schools.
- English Comprehension, Maths, Creative & Persuasive Writing, Reasoning (VR & NVR) and bonus material.
- Written and multiple-choice formats.
- Solutions to real past papers from leading schools - with example answers, discussions and full working.
- Individual marking and feedback available for your child's work.
- Cancel at any time.
- Ideal for children in Years 5 & 6.

"I passed the exam, most of which was because of your help! I don't have an actual tutor like most of my friends, but I feel so lucky to have your papers every week. I think you are the best tutor!" - David Tao, 11

WWW.11PLUSLIFELINE.COM